Violet's Life Lessons:

Growing Toward God

Cultivating Your Life of Faith

Written by
Wendy Witherow
and Beverly Elliott

Franklin, Tennessee

Published by Mission City Press, Inc.

Illustrations: Kelly Pulley
Cover Design: Richmond & Williams, Nashville, Tennessee
Cover Photography: Michelle Grisco Photography, West Covina, California
Typesetting: BookSetters, Bowling Green, Kentucky

 Note: Where there are italics within a verse of Scripture, emphasis is added by the authors.

For more information, write to Mission City Press at 202 Second Avenue South, Franklin, Tennessee 37064, or visit our Web Site at www.alifeoffaith.com.

Library of Congress Catalog Card Number: 2007922298
Beverly Elliott, Wendy Witherow
Violet's Life Lessons: Growing Toward God
ISBN 10: 1-928749-62-3
ISBN 13: 978-1-928749-62-2

Printed in the United States of America
1 2 3 4 5 6 7 8 — 12 11 10 09 08 07

CONTENTS

Welcome to *Violet's Life Lessons: Growing Toward God*

At the heart of the *A Life of Faith: Violet Travilla* book series, readers discover an endearing story of a fourteen-year-old girl's day-by-day journey of personal and spiritual growth, which is what a life of faith is really all about—the minutes and hours of each day that make up the weeks, months, and years of our lives. It's tending to our spiritual lives each day, side by side with our Heavenly Father and Friend, looking to Him for guidance, fellowship, freedom, and growth.

Violet's faith journey is probably not so unlike your own. Many readers of the *Violet Travilla* book series have shared how Violet's experiences have encouraged them:

> *The Violet books are wonderful! They have many life lessons in them. I really enjoy reading about someone so young having so much faith and courage. She is an inspiration to us all. —Ashley, age 11*

> *I really like the books and they make me want to live a life of faith just like her. —Jennifer, age 14*

> *After reading the Violet books, I felt better about growing up. —Heidi, age 15*

> *I think Violet is a wonderful role model for girls! She is a kind and compassionate girl who, I think, a lot of us can relate to. After I read the first Violet book, I put Violet on my mental list of good role models. —Hannah, age 11*

This study guide simply endeavors to help you grow toward God and to cultivate your life of faith in Him, just as Violet did. The main focus of the teaching will center on the lovely analogy of gardening, which beautifully illustrates many spiritual principles about our growth in Christ. We want this study to be informative and fun, and to be an avenue for you to flourish in your own life of faith!

As you read through the *Violet Travilla* book series and study her life, you see how Vi's spiritual life steadily grows and unfolds. First, God prepared the soil of Vi's heart through trials and sufferings. Next, spiritual seeds were planted in her heart through loved ones. Then, the tender stalk and early heads of grain were nourished through her diligence to study God's Word and align her life accordingly.

Vi's openness to God created a rich, fertile soil for the seed of the life of Christ to grow, mature, and produce a very fruitful harvest through her. This harvest comes forth in Vi's life through her work at an inner-city mission called Samaritan House, a place of ministry she founded, which became her harvest field. You too, like Vi, can enjoy the incredible thrill of bearing fruit for Christ in your very own harvest field. But there is a growth process in reaching this place of maturity. It is an exciting, wonderful process of growing toward God, and this study guide will help lead you on your own unique garden path with the Master Gardener Himself.

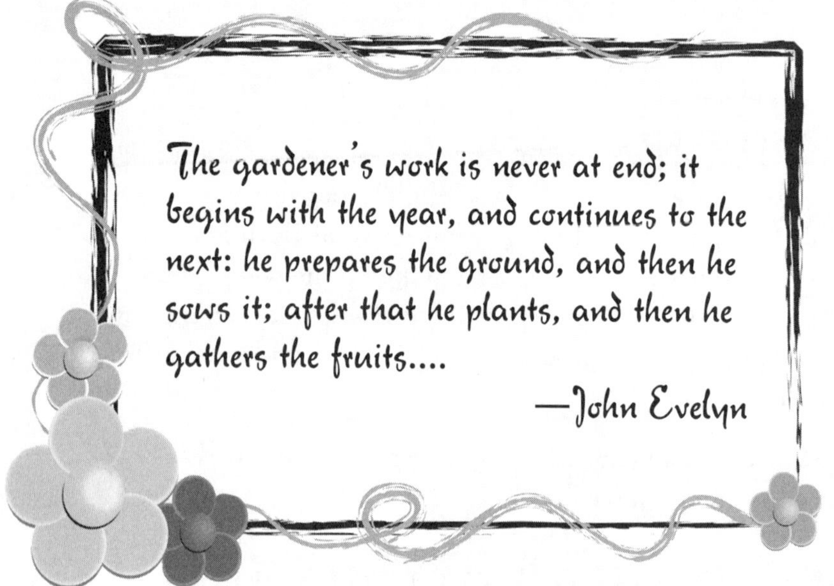

The gardener's work is never at end; it begins with the year, and continues to the next: he prepares the ground, and then he sows it; after that he plants, and then he gathers the fruits....
—John Evelyn

Growing Toward God—the heart's impassioned desire of every faithful soul chasing after a life of faith in Christ. From the newest child of God to the most seasoned of God's saints, we never stop growing toward the One who created us and who knows our every thought and dream, the One who sees the beginning and ending of each life, and the One who is the Author and Perfecter of our faith.

No matter where you are in your faith growth with God, we invite you to read on and open your heart to learning more about this wondrous, lifelong process of growing toward the Lover of your soul—God Almighty. So don those gardening gloves, pick up that hoe, and let's dig into God's Word!

How to Use This Study Guide

- Supplies: colored pencils, Bible, dictionary, thesaurus, and a journal (optional)
- Start each lesson with prayer. Ask the Holy Spirit, who guides you into all truth (John 16:13), to give you wisdom and understanding to help you apply these truths to your life. Read each Scripture slowly, maybe two times, to really grasp the meaning.

- It would be helpful to remove yourself to a quiet place as you work through the lessons. Vi loved to steal away with her Bible, journal, and sketchbook to some remote place without distractions, such as the dock at the lake, where she could focus on hearing the Lord speak to her.
- Look for the symbol of the shovel next to the passages of Scripture where you will be digging deeper. Pretend you are digging for precious treasures. Let your colored pencils be your spade and shovel to help you uncover hidden truths. We will give you some instruction on what to mark in your passages, but feel free to do your own excavating. Mark any repetitive words, main ideas, promises, and other treasures you may find. Be creative. Use your own colors and symbols and mark as much as you want.
- Extra information about agriculture during Bible times can be found in the Appendix at the end of the study. We recommend that you read through this information before you begin your study, as it will help make the Scriptures come to life and add wonderful insight to your gardening journey.

A Word About the Master Gardener

In this study guide we use the term "Master Gardener" to refer to God as the one who oversees our spiritual growth and who has expert knowledge when it comes to working in the soil of our hearts and making truth and joy grow and flourish in our lives.

In the world of horticulture, a master gardener is an individual who receives specialized training in the knowledge of cultivating all types of plants. Master gardeners are required to complete a minimum of 40 hours of classroom instruction where they become experts in their area of plant health and growth. But it doesn't stop there. The responsibility which comes from the privilege of knowledge is sharing it with others. A master gardener then takes this acquired wisdom and skill and commits to another 40 hours of volunteer service to the community through teaching and helping others learn how to garden and grow beautiful plants.

As we study extensively under the tutorage of our own divine Master Gardener, we too can learn the secrets of cultivating our spiritual lives. The joy and excitement of growing toward God inspires us likewise to go out into our communities and harvest fields and to teach others these principles of growing toward God.

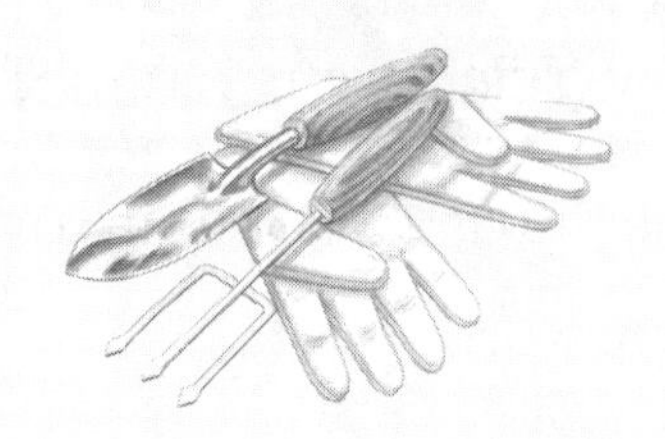

Lesson One

In the Beginning . . . There Was a Garden

Let's begin our gardening journey together by standing at the gate of the most famous garden in all of history—the Garden of Eden! When God created the heavens and the earth, one of the first things He did was to plant a divine garden. He placed Adam and Eve in this garden to live so they could enjoy it. Let's peer inside and try to imagine what God's own garden must have looked like as you read the following verses:

> Now the Lord God had planted a garden in the east, in Eden; and there he put the man he had formed. And the Lord God made all kinds of trees grow out of the ground—trees that were pleasing to the eye and good for food. In the middle of the garden were the tree of life and the tree of the knowledge of good and evil. A river watering the garden flowed from Eden; from there it was separated into four headwaters.
>
> —Genesis 2:8-10

Isn't it a special token of God's love that He created such a lush and beautiful garden for Adam and Eve to dwell? What a wondrous moment it must have been for Adam when he took his first step into that magnificent place! Imagine the possibilities of what this divine garden might have been like. What if the sunflowers grew as tall as trees? Perhaps the rose petals were the size of your hand. Imagine that you are the first human being on God's brand-new earth, and your new home is nothing less than a garden of paradise. So just close your eyes and imagine the breathtaking beauty of this garden of paradise. Write your own creative description of the Garden of Eden below:

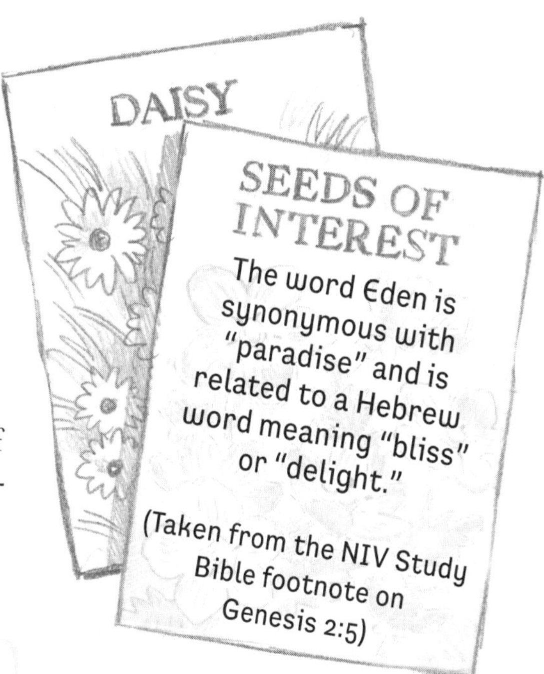

DAISY
SEEDS OF INTEREST
The word Eden is synonymous with "paradise" and is related to a Hebrew word meaning "bliss" or "delight."
(Taken from the NIV Study Bible footnote on Genesis 2:5)

Go back and slowly re-read the verses from Genesis 2. Using your colored pencils, draw a green triangle around the word "tree" each time it appears. Then answer the following:

1. The passage says that there were "all kinds of trees" growing in the garden. What two things does this passage say about those particular trees?

Treels that were plesing to the eye and good for food.

Our Master Gardener loves to bless His children with very good things. He made Adam and Eve's home in the garden very pleasing to all of their senses.

2. The tree of life must have been different from the other trees. It wasn't there just to provide food. What do you think made the tree of life special? How could it have been different from the other trees? (Don't be afraid to brainstorm your ideas and use your imagination.)

The tree of life was special because it gave life and happiness. It made life happy.

The tree of life is said to represent the presence of God in the garden. Notice it was located in the center of the Garden of Eden. This symbolized that God was the core or center of Adam and Eve's life and existence in the garden. God saw fit to supply everything Adam and Eve would need for an abundant life in the Garden of Eden.

Now let's look at another passage. Once again, draw a green triangle around the word "tree" each time is appears:

> THE LORD GOD TOOK THE MAN AND PUT HIM IN THE GARDEN OF EDEN TO WORK IT AND TAKE CARE OF IT. AND THE LORD GOD COMMANDED THE MAN, "YOU ARE FREE TO EAT FROM ANY TREE IN THE GARDEN; BUT YOU MUST NOT EAT FROM THE TREE OF THE KNOWLEDGE OF GOOD AND EVIL, FOR WHEN YOU EAT OF IT YOU WILL SURELY DIE."
>
> —GENESIS 2:15-17

1. What special assignment was Adam given in the garden?

To work it and take care of it.

This was a shared assignment between God and Adam. There is a shared joy in working together. This God-given responsibility is the same for us today as it was for Adam then. Only we are to tend and care for the garden of our hearts—our spiritual lives. Like Adam, we too share the joy of this work with our Master Gardener. This joy is called "communion," and it means we enjoy sweet friendship and closeness with God. In the days ahead, as we study gardening and how it relates to our own spiritual growth, we can take comfort in knowing that God has always been the Master Gardener—and He is to this very day. He gently works alongside us tending to every aspect of our spiritual growth in the gardens of our hearts.

2. What one thing did God ask Adam and Eve not to do?

To eat from tree of knowledge.

Joy

God, their perfect Heavenly Father, lovingly established boundaries for Adam and Eve—boundaries that were good and were meant to protect their intimate fellowship with God and the life they enjoyed in the garden. He also lovingly gave them the freedom to choose their own way. As long as they chose to come under God's good plan, Adam and Eve were in complete oneness with God and experienced unbroken fellowship with Him. All of their emotional, spiritual, and physical needs were met and they lived in a state of never-ending joy.

Like Adam and Eve, we also have been given a choice. We too can experience life and unbroken fellowship with God through Christ, who will now stand as the tree of life in the middle of the garden of our hearts. We only have to ask.

REFLECTION:

Have you invited Jesus to be your Savior and tree of life? Will you choose to receive from Him everything you need for life and intimate fellowship with the Father? Will you entrust your heart to the One who died to bring your garden to life? If you have already received Christ as Savior, give thanks to Him and anticipate the beautiful plantings the two of you will grow together throughout this study. If you have not invited Jesus to be your Lord, why not invite Him into your heart right now? Here is a simple prayer you can pray to receive Christ as your Lord.

Dear Master Gardener,

I want my heart to be a garden of friendship and communion with You. But because of my sins, my heart is full of weeds, thistles, rocks, and dry places.

I have often made wrong choices, but I want to change. I am sorry for my sins and I pray that You will forgive me for them. I accept the free gift of Jesus' death on the Cross in my place. I believe that Jesus died for my sins and was raised from the dead. I invite You—Father, Son, and Holy Spirit— to come live inside my heart and change me for the better. I give my life to You right now, and I ask that from this day forth, You would help me to follow You, to love You more and more, and to get to know You better. I want to grow toward You. Take my overgrown, weedy garden and restore it to proper growth and life. Amen.

Please refer to Section 6 in the Appendix to learn more about your new life in Christ.

Vi's Gardening Tip:

In His wisdom and love, your Master Gardener has established good guidelines for you, just as He did for Adam and Eve in the Garden of Eden. These guidelines, when followed, serve to keep the tree of life—Christ—growing strong and healthy in the center of your garden. As you move forward in this study and further explore some of these good guidelines, keep in mind that they are all part of God's good plan to maintain and nurture life in your garden.

There is a garden in every childhood, an enchanted place where colors are brighter, the air softer, and the morning more fragrant than ever again.

—Elizabeth Lawrence

Lesson Two

The Garden of Your Heart

Gardens are meant to be enjoyed. They are places of sweet communion and restoration. Have you ever sat in the midst of a peaceful garden and allowed the fragrance and colorful hues of the flowers to fill up your senses? In such a soothing environment, it's so easy to commune with God and enjoy calming refreshment for your soul.

Likewise, the Garden of Eden was a place of beauty and communion enjoyed by God and Adam and Eve. We even read in Genesis 3:8 that God walked in the Garden. We can imagine that God took great pleasure in this garden home. Here He fellowshipped with Adam and Eve and enjoyed being with them. They delighted in each other.

However, when Adam and Eve disobeyed God and ate from the wrong tree (Genesis 3:6), their precious relationship with God was disrupted. This choice caused them to lose their oneness with God, and they became independent and wise in their own eyes (prideful), which ultimately resulted in their being cast out of the Garden of Eden.

But our loving Master Gardener would not allow this garden of sweet communion to be ruined. In His perfect time, He sent His Son, Jesus, to die to remove the power of sin that separates us from God. God, through Jesus, has restored His precious garden of communion. It's not a physical place anymore as the Garden of Eden was. Now, intimate fellowship and sheer enjoyment with God happens within the garden of our hearts. Through the resurrected life of Christ living within us, we can have the continual abiding presence of God—our garden experience—whenever and wherever we may be. God finds great pleasure in resting or dwelling in the garden of your soul and being with you. Now, He walks with you in the garden of your heart as He walked with Adam and Eve in the Garden of Eden. He said in 2 Corinthians 6:16b, "I will *dwell* in them and *walk* among them; and I will be their God, and they shall be My people" (New American Standard Bible).

Reflection:

Imagine what a beautiful place God will create for you in your heart's garden! Your Master Gardener is divinely skilled in creating and designing exquisite gardens. Remember the splendor of the Garden of Eden! Look back at the beginning of Lesson 1. What was the definition of the word "Eden"? Your Master Gardener will create a paradise of bliss and delight in the garden of your heart for both of you to enjoy.

No matter how desolate and barren your garden may appear, there is great hope for you. He can turn an empty and dry heart into a green and flourishing garden and make it shout with joy! Let's look at the following Scripture and see what miracles God can do for you.

> The Lord will surely comfort Zion and will look with compassion on all her ruins; he will make her deserts like Eden, her wastelands like the garden of the Lord. Joy and gladness will be found in her, thanksgiving and the sound of singing.
>
> —Isaiah 51:3

Draw a flower around the words that describe the joy found in the Lord's garden.

What part of this passage brings hope to you and why?

Comfort, Gladness, and sound of singing all bring me hope because I want does thing cause I love them!

Your Master Gardener will create for you a beautiful, one-of-a-kind spiritual garden full of joy, gladness, fragrance, and singing! You will have YOUR OWN distinct flowers and trees growing in your garden. Your garden will have ITS OWN sweet, "exclusive" fragrance that is shared by none other. What a wonderful thought! In Song of Songs 4:16, the maiden says,

AWAKE, NORTH WIND, AND COME, SOUTH WIND! BLOW ON MY GARDEN, THAT ITS FRAGRANCE MAY SPREAD ABROAD.

—SONG OF SONGS 4:16

Envision the garden of your heart. Refer to "Flowers of the Bible" in Section 4 of the Appendix. What flowers would you like to grow in your heart's garden? Choose some from this list (or add your own) and write them down below. What's your garden's unique fragrance? Give your special fragrance a name! Give a brief explanation of your choices:

Tulip

Grape

Anemone

laundry

Cyclamen

strawberry

Ask your Master Gardener to make your spiritual garden as fragrant as these flowers. Pray that the wind of His Holy Spirit would blow the fragrance of joy from your garden abroad to others.

Vi's Gardening Tip:

In conclusion of today's study, look back at Isaiah 51:3 and notice there is singing in the garden.

We can experience the thrill of knowing that God is walking and singing with joy and gladness in the garden of our souls, and we can raise our voices to join His with a song of thanksgiving!

As you think about the garden of your heart and the joy of fellowshipping with God, take some time to pen your own special garden song. Need help getting started? Look up Psalm 145 and use it as a model for your own song of joy and thanksgiving for the One who loves you!

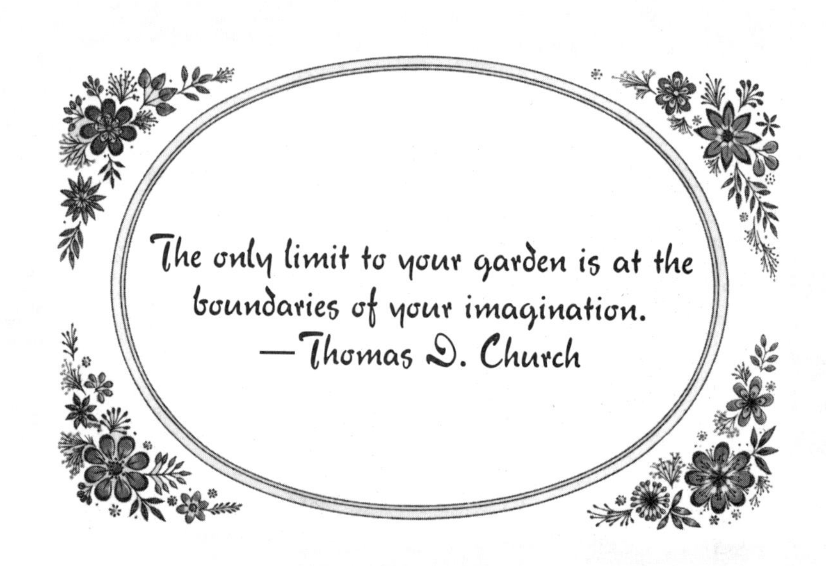

The only limit to your garden is at the boundaries of your imagination.
—Thomas D. Church

Lesson Three

Ready the Soil

You've entrusted your heart to the Master Gardner and you've partnered with Him in this joyful work. Now it's time to try your hand at gardening in the soil of your heart. You've "picked" the type of plants and flowers you'd like to grow, and the little seeds hold the promise of fragrant-smelling flowers or fresh-tasting produce. You can hardly wait to get the seeds in the soil so that your gardening adventure can get underway. But as with much of life, there is always a delicate, systematic process and timing for all things. You know that the seeds probably won't grow overnight, but did you know that there must be certain conditions in the soil for your seeds to thrive? So what is the first course of action you should take to assure the best-producing crop from your seeds? Why, readying the soil, of course!

It is a well-known fact that the secret to growing a successful garden begins with the soil. If there is a proper balance of nutrients in the soil, such as potassium, nitrogen, and phosphorus, plants will grow strong and healthy. Before planting their crops, skilled, serious gardeners take samples of the soil to check for the proportions of minerals and nutrients and other things. To get an accurate reading, they must dig at least *12 inches deep* because surface soil can give a false reading. The same is true with the soil of our hearts. We must allow the truths of God's Word to penetrate deep within us.

Like a wise gardener, if we want our lives to bear stunning flowers and ripe, juicy fruit for Jesus, we too must test the soil of our own hearts to see what the conditions are and what attention is needed.

To begin our study on soil, look up 2 Corinthians 13:5 and write it below. This verse shows us the importance of taking a "soil sample."

Examine yourselves as to whether you are in the faith. Test yourselves. Do you not know yourselves, that Jesus Christ is in you?– unless indeed that you are disqualified.

God's Word encourages us to examine and test ourselves to make sure that we are "in the faith." As we begin our gardening adventure together, this is our first step—examining our own hearts. We will do this by "readying the soil" and looking at the types of "soil" that can hinder not only the growth of a garden, but the growth of the spiritual garden in our hearts.

REFLECTION:

Why is readying the soil so important to gardening?

Because it will grow strong and healthy.

Why is readying the soil of our hearts so important to our spiritual growth?

So Gods word will (the truth) penetrate deep.

Let's read an insightful parable Jesus taught, which will be the basis of the next four lessons:

Jesus taught a parable in Matthew 13 that compared the different conditions of our hearts to different types of soil.

The Parable of the Sower

SEEDS OF INTEREST

Agriculture in Bible Days

In Bible days, people were agriculturists; they made their living from the land. God spoke to them in gardening terms because He knew they would understand. In the parable of the sower, the seed is sown by hand. The sower walks across the field scattering handfuls of seed from a container until the entire field is covered. See "Planting or Sowing" in Section 2 of the Appendix.

That same day Jesus went out of the house and sat by the lake. Such large crowds gathered around him that he got into a boat and sat in it, while all the people stood on the shore. Then he told them many things in parables, saying: "A farmer went out to sow his seed. As he was scattering the seed, some fell along the path, and the birds came and ate it up. Some fell on rocky places, where it did not have much soil. It sprang up quickly, because the soil was shallow. But when the sun came up, the plants were scorched, and they withered because they had no root. Other seed fell among thorns, which grew up and choked the plants. Still other seed fell on good soil, where it produced a crop—a hundred, sixty or thirty times what was sown. He who has ears, let him hear."

—Matthew 13:1-9

There are four types of soil described in this passage. Fill out the following graph to chart the four types of soil:

Where the seed was sown (or type of soil):	**What happened to the seed or plant:**
1. The path	The birds ate it up.
2. Rocky places	It sprang up quickly.
3. Thorns	~~[illegible]~~ Choked the plants.
4. Good soil	A hundred, sixty, or thirty-what was sown. (crop)

Take a look at the chart. Understanding these four types of soil is foundational for our spiritual growth. Therefore, we will look in-depth at each type of soil over the next four lessons. In doing so, we will also examine the condition of our own hearts and ready the soil for the spiritual seeds of blessing!

Vi's Gardening Tip:

One of the fastest ways to get an accurate "soil sample" from your heart is to ask a parent or trusted adult to be honest with you. Oftentimes, older mentors in our lives can see things about our character more clearly than we can see for ourselves. So don't be afraid to ask for an "outside" perspective. But be ready to listen with ears that can hear.

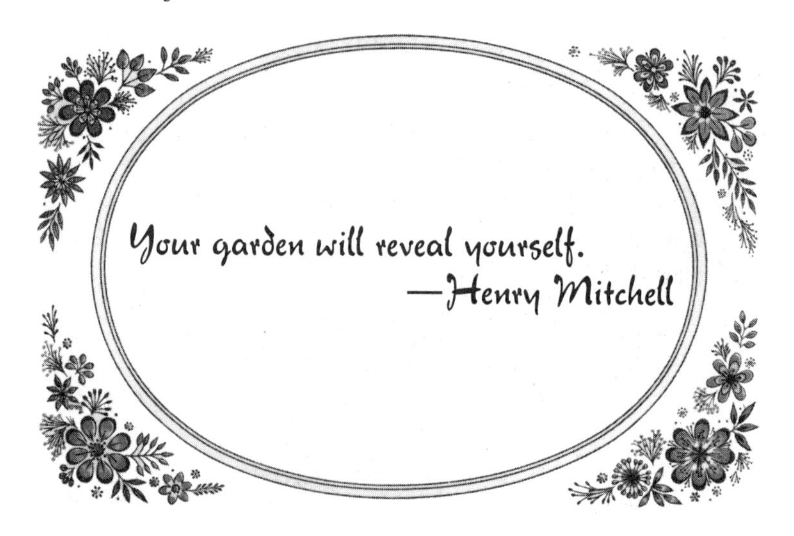

Your garden will reveal yourself.
—Henry Mitchell

Lesson Four

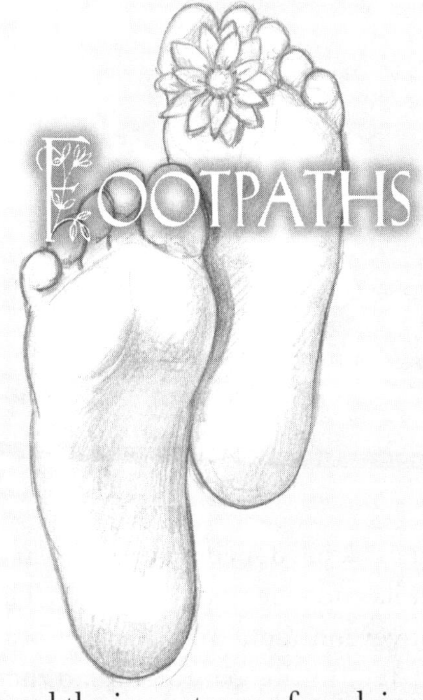

Footpaths

In the previous lesson we learned the importance of readying the soil of our hearts. Now let's begin to explore how we can keep our heart's soil soft and fertile. Let's take a closer look at Jesus's parable in Matthew 13.

> A FARMER WENT OUT TO SOW HIS SEED. AS HE WAS SCATTERING THE SEED, SOME FELL ALONG THE PATH, AND THE BIRDS CAME AND ATE IT UP.
>
> —MATTHEW 13:3-4

The seed that fell along the path is the first soil we will examine. Think about a common pathway upon which you have walked. The earth beneath you is solid, hard, and immovable. The seed that "fell along the path" fell upon soil that had become hard and firmly packed down due to travel—the passage of feet, horses and chariots, and other means of transportation. The soil on a footpath is usually virtually impenetrable to seed because it has become "hard as a rock." The seeds are left lying in the open where the birds can see them and snatch them up. The birds represent the enemy of our souls, Satan. He is always ready to snatch the seeds of God's truth away from our hearts. If the soil of our hearts is hard, then God's seeds will not implant, and Satan will snatch away the truth that Christ is trying to sow into our lives. Now look up Matthew 13:19, which explains the meaning of the hardened paths, and write it below:

When anyone hears the word of the kingdom and does not understand it, then the wicked one comes and snatches away what was sown in his heart. This is he who received seed by the wayside.

The hardened footpath represents a hardened heart—a heart that will not listen and is not teachable—a heart that hears but has no true understanding. The soil of this heart is hardened by pride, sin, and unbelief. It is overconfident and thinks it is already wise. Jesus addressed this hardened condition after He taught this parable. Read the following passages carefully. Using your colored pencils, underline the words "hear" or "hearing" in purple and circle the words "understand" or "understanding" in green.

> In them is fulfilled the prophecy of Isaiah: "You will be ever hearing but never understanding; you will be ever seeing but never perceiving. For this people's heart has become calloused; they hardly hear with their ears, and they have closed their eyes. Otherwise they might see with their eyes, hear with their ears, understand with their hearts and turn, and I would heal them."
>
> —Matthew 13:14-15

From reading this parable, what do you think the difference is between hearing and understanding?

The difference is that hearing is just hearing and not understanding. Understanding is not hearing you just understand

Hearing the Word of Truth is not enough. A heart that only hears the Word has hardened soil that prevents God's truth from going deep enough into the heart to take root. There is, therefore, no change in our lives. The Word cannot affect our attitude, thoughts, and behavior. Spiritual understanding happens when our heart's soil is soft to allow God's Word to go deep and take root. Then the "eyes of our heart" are opened (spiritual understanding) and we are transformed. Our lives are changed through receiving God's powerful, healing, and life-giving touch through His Word. An example of "hearing without understanding" would be listening to a sermon on Sunday morning and then leaving without allowing the message to have any impact on your life.

It's insightful to note that footpaths of the heart become calloused and hardened due to *regular and consistent* travel of rebellion and pride down the same path. It's time to examine your soil to see where your hardened footpaths are. Here are the signs of hardened ground in your heart:

- Easily get defensive and unable to listen to and receive counsel or correction from parents or others in positions of authority.
- Think more of self than others (selfish attitude). For instance, when you're making weekend plans with friends, are you willing to do what they suggest, or do you insist on doing what you want to do?
- Deceptive belief that you know more than others. Are you able to hear others' opinions without needing to prove your own point of view?
- Have difficulty seeing your own faults and believing you might need to grow in some areas.
- Seldom take time to pray and read the Bible to receive from the Lord.

Look back at the list of symptoms of hardened ground. Spend a few minutes and ask the Master Gardener to reveal stubborn or hardened areas you might observe in your own heart. Write what your Master Gardener shows you below:

Why are these footpaths dangerous to your spiritual growth?

God is a forgiving, redeeming, and loving Father. He wants the soil of your heart to be soft and fertile so that the seed of His truth can flourish and grow strong within you. The most effective way to soften hard soil is with water. If there are hardened places in the soil of your heart, you can "water" the soil through the sweet act of repentance. Acts 3:19 says, "Repent, then, and turn to God, so that your sins may be wiped out, that times of refreshing may come from the Lord."

To *repent* means to turn away from sin and to turn fully back to God. Turning from sin means you don't want to do it anymore, and turning to God means you trust Him to get it out of your life. He will forgive your sin, wipe it out, and send you a refreshing touch that will revive your soul and soften your heart. He will take that hard footpath and turn it into a soft, fragrant flower bed for many to enjoy!

Now let's allow the refreshing rain of God to come and pour on those hard areas of your heart through repentance. Take each area you have written above in the Reflection section. Ask God to forgive you of this pattern or struggle and then make a choice to walk on a different path. You may find yourself trodding down those old established paths without even knowing it. But each time you catch yourself, repent and turn back to God. In doing this, you will be establishing new patterns and eventually those old paths will disappear due to lack of use. Your Master Gardener is very patient and understanding toward you. Allow Him to help you. You can't do it on your own. Look to Him and be patient with yourself.

Another method that gardeners use to soften soil is to fertilize it with compost (dead and decaying plant or animal material). Look up James 1:21 and write it below. See if you can find the key quality in this passage that will fertilize your soil. Circle it:

As you see, humility is the fertilizer necessary for soft soil in your heart. Look up the word "humility" in your dictionary and write the meaning below:

We all must work "humility" into the soil of our hearts. A humble heart is teachable and able to hear and understand. It recognizes quickly when it is wrong and is quick to repent. For example, have you ever realized you did something wrong and felt really bad about it, and then immediately prayed about it? That's a tender heart and this soft soil makes it easy for God's Word to be implanted.

Vi's Gardening Tip:

Psalm 51 portrays a beautiful representation of a repentant and humble heart. Open up your Bible and turn to this Psalm. Read through it and then make note of the highlights below. These suggestions will help to keep your heart tender toward God.

- Know that God is full of tender mercy toward you (verse 1). If you sin and repent, God is quick to forgive you and is compassionate toward your weaknesses.
- Ask God to forgive your hardened heart and to wash and cleanse you in His great mercy (verses 2, 3, and 7).
- Ask God to create in you a pure and tender heart and a steadfast, loyal spirit (verse 10).
- Ask God to help you be humble and to be quick to repent. He delights in such tender soil (verse 17).
- Praise and thank Him for His abounding forgiveness and mercy (verse 15).

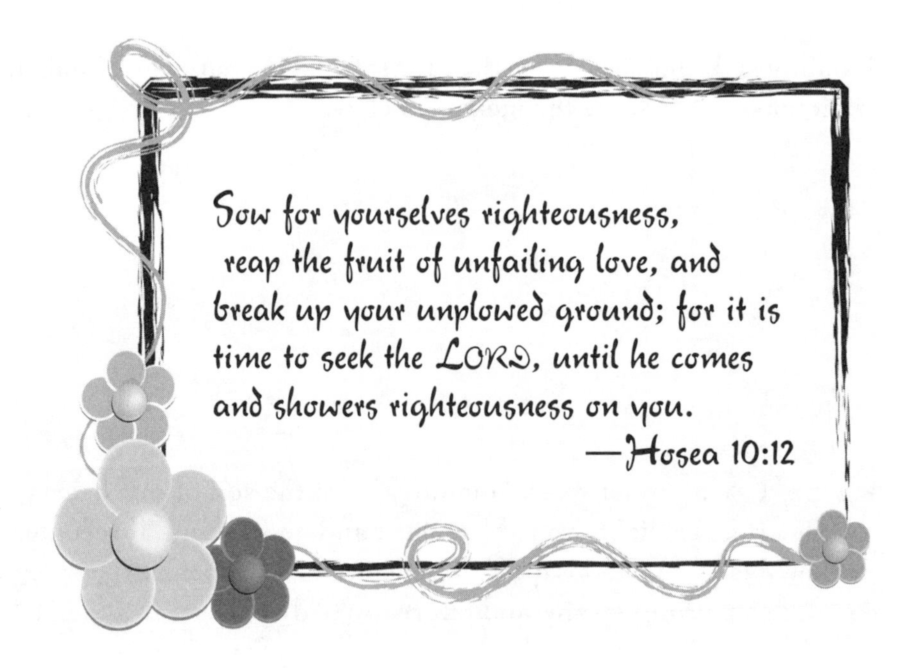

Sow for yourselves righteousness,
reap the fruit of unfailing love, and
break up your unplowed ground; for it is
time to seek the LORD, until he comes
and showers righteousness on you.
—Hosea 10:12

Lesson Five

Next we'll turn our attention to the stony, rocky soil. Let's read Matthew 13:5-6:

> SOME FELL ON *ROCKY PLACES,* WHERE IT DID NOT HAVE MUCH SOIL. IT SPRANG UP QUICKLY, BECAUSE THE SOIL WAS SHALLOW. BUT WHEN THE SUN CAME UP, THE PLANTS WERE SCORCHED, AND THEY WITHERED BECAUSE THEY HAD NO ROOT.
>
> —MATTHEW 13:5-6

Rocky soil allows the seed to penetrate, but only near the surface. Because of the rocks, the seed cannot grow roots deep enough to sustain itself. When the tender plant becomes exposed to the heat of the sun, its roots aren't deep enough to receive water and nourishment so the tender shoot shrivels up and dies. Matthew 13:20-21 explains the spiritual meaning of the rocky soil. Look up the verses and write them below:

As you can see, this type of soil represents a heart which hears God's Word and receives it with joy, but never acts on it to allow the Word to go deep and take root. This is a shallow Christian, because the soil is shallow. When the heat of trials and tribulations comes, the plants cannot endure, because they are not sufficiently rooted.

It's time to examine your heart for this type of rocky, shallow soil. Is there a command in the Bible that you are not acting upon? Think about this carefully. There are many spiritual truths in God's Word that are meant to help each of us live a balanced, happy life—God's truths provide a solid foundation for us, an anchor for the soul. However, if we do not act upon the Word, we will live shallow lives, and that is bad news, especially when the storms of life hit!

You see, the result of living a shallow Christian life is devastating. Read the following passage. These are the words of Jesus concerning this type of soil. Using your colored pencils, underline in red what happens to the house built on sand:

> BUT EVERYONE WHO HEARS THESE WORDS OF MINE AND DOES NOT PUT THEM INTO PRACTICE IS LIKE A FOOLISH MAN WHO BUILT HIS HOUSE ON SAND. THE RAIN CAME DOWN, THE STREAMS ROSE, AND THE WINDS BLEW AND BEAT AGAINST THAT HOUSE, AND IT FELL WITH A GREAT CRASH.
>
> —MATTHEW 7:26-27

In our previous lesson we learned that we must not just hear God's Word, but we must understand His Word and allow it to go deep enough to change our hearts. This heart transformation will then produce in us the faith and desire to apply His words to our lives, or as the above passage says, "to put them into practice." If we obey God's Word, then we will be securely anchored on a solid foundation. If not, we are like the foolish man above. Shallow, sandy soil is not good for houses or plants. James 1:22 says, "Do not merely listen to the word, and so deceive yourselves. Do what it says."

What truths in God's Word are you struggling to live out? It may be something very obvious, like disobeying authorities or lying, or it may be more subtle, like harboring a disrespectful attitude toward a parent even if you do as he or she asks. This "hidden" struggle matters to God. He sees beyond outward obedience. Review the following list of symptoms and then answer the questions that come after it:

A Shallow Heart

- Refuses to obey God's Word in a certain area.
- Responds enthusiastically to God's Word when caught up in the emotional rush, but cannot follow through when the emotions fade and the going gets tough. For instance, you attend church camp and have a "mountaintop experience," but two weeks later (when the emotional high is gone) you drift back into living a shallow Christian life.
- Makes a superficial (shallow) commitment to the gospel, which does not require letting go of selfish desires.
- Entertains doubts that can undermine faith and allow for a shallow implanting of God's Word.
- Is easily swayed by the opinions of others instead of being firmly rooted in the truth of God's Word.

Reflection:

1. Spend a few minutes and ask the Master Gardener to reveal any symptoms of rocky soil in your heart. Write your thoughts below:

2. In your own words, explain what you think it means to be a "shallow" Christian, and why living a "shallow" Christian life is dangerous:

Pray and ask the Lord to help you desire to obey His Words. Then *choose* to do it! With God's help and your desire to obey, you can remove these pebbles one by one! He promises to lead you into victory, so cast your cares upon Him and allow Him to change your heart. Philippians 4:13 says, "I can do everything through him who gives me strength."

Vi's Gardening Tip:

We will always have some rocks and pebbles in our soil. But, we must not grow weary in being diligent to rake them out regularly. Here are some tips to remove those pesky rocks:

- ❀ Make a determined decision to obey God in an area of disobedience in your life. Get an adult mentor or friend to pray for you in this area of struggle.
- ❀ Discipline yourself to take time each day to read God's Word and to pray for faith to believe and obey what you read (Romans 10:17).
- ❀ Go to your garden of communion and spend time with your Master Gardener.
- ❀ Ask the Master Gardener to reveal His love for you. Talk to Him. Look into His face and receive His perfect, unconditional love for you.

A person's character and their garden both reflect the amount of weeding that was done during the growing season.
—Author Unknown

If you've ever been pricked by a thorn, you know how much it stings! Let's see what thorns will do to our hearts. Read Matthew 13:7.

> OTHER SEED FELL AMONG THORNS, WHICH GREW UP AND CHOKED THE PLANTS.
>
> —MATTHEW 13:7

This third type of soil—thorny soil—allowed the seed to take root and grow, possibly for a while, but soon the thorns began to grow along with the plant, overtaking the garden and choking out the good seed.

In terms of our spiritual growth, this type of soil produces heartbreaking results. Here's how it happens: A believer starts out with good soil in her heart. God's good seed is sown, a root is established, and it begins to grow. Just when it seems that she is growing toward God and everything is fine, something happens—she forgets to tend to the weeds and thistles. Soon they have grown big enough to choke out the good and precious plants that have grown up from God's seed.

If you've ever worked in a garden, you know how fast the weeds grow—almost overnight! The weedy roots crowd out the good roots and the good plant dies. That's why it is so important to *weed your garden regularly and diligently*. When preparing soil for a garden, if any roots are left from grass or other weeds, they will grow back and choke out the newly planted foliage.

Watch for thorns in the garden of your heart! What exactly are the thorns you need to be aware of? *A thorn is anything that begins to get your focus off of the goodness, mercy, and love of the Lord.* It is spiritual clutter; it distracts! A thorn will begin to sap you of your peace, your energy, and your joy. The most common thorns we struggle with are worry and fear. For instance, worrying about how you look or fearing that you won't be accepted at school.

Look up Matthew 13:22 and write it down below. This passage explains the spiritual meaning of the thorny soil.

What thorns can you identify in your garden which might be choking out the life of Christ growing there and preventing you from becoming a fruitful plant for the Lord? Which consumes you—the kingdom of God or the things of the world? Remember, a thorn represents anything that is distracting your focus away from Christ.

Consider the following list of potential "thorns" as you examine your heart:

- Worries and cares of the world that cause anxiety and fear (e.g., losing sleep worrying that a classmate is upset with you or anxious thoughts about a conflict at school).
- Discontentment with what you have, always wanting more, and believing that riches will make you happy (e.g., needing the latest and greatest fashions, electronics, etc.).
- Desire for peer approval or success at all costs (e.g., treating others poorly in order to fit in with a certain group of friends).
- Priorities out of whack—worldly interests taking priority over spiritual interests (e.g., missing youth group gatherings to watch your favorite TV show).

Reflection:

1. Are there any "thorns" (or worries) in your heart that you can identify? Maybe you worry too much about what you wear to school and how you look. Write your thoughts below:

2. How might those thorns be stunting your spiritual growth?

If you feel overwhelmed by the worries and cares of this life, allow the following Scripture passage to soak into your soil to restore your peace and joy in Jesus again. First, underline in red every time you read about the thorn of worry. In green, underline every passage which speaks of God's faithful provision for you or His creation. Finally, in blue, underline the Lord's command (near the end of the passage) that will help get rid of these thorns of worry. Try to memorize a portion of the passage. When we hide God's Word in our hearts, it transforms our thoughts and actions and helps us to grow.

Therefore I tell you, do not worry about your life, what you will eat or drink; or about your body, what you will wear. Is not life more important than food, and the body more important than clothes? Look at the birds of the air; they do not sow or reap or store away in barns, and yet your heavenly Father feeds them. Are you not much more valuable than they? Who of you by worrying can add a single hour to his life? And why do you worry about clothes? See how the lilies of the field grow. They do not labor or spin. Yet I tell you that not even Solomon in all his splendor was dressed like one of these. If that is how God clothes the grass of the field, which is here today and tomorrow is thrown into the fire, will he not much more clothe you, O you of little faith? So do not worry, saying, "What shall we eat?" or "What shall we drink?"or "What shall we wear?" For the pagans run after all these things, and your heavenly Father knows that you need them. But seek first his kingdom and his righteousness, and all these things will be given to you as well. Therefore do not worry about tomorrow, for tomorrow will worry about itself. Each day has enough trouble of its own.

—Matthew 6:25-34

After reading the above passage, list some reasons why you shouldn't worry about the cares you listed earlier:

Some people believe that the lilies of the field mentioned in Matthew 6 could have been the wide variety of wildflowers that bloomed on the hillsides in Israel in the spring, such as anemones, daisies, poppies, rockrose, or thorny broom. The hillside where Jesus spoke to the crowds, somewhere near the Sea of Galilee, was probably robed in a spectacular array of color from reds and purples to pink, white, and yellow. Jesus had only to wave His hand to direct the crowd's attention to these beautifully clothed wildflowers to illustrate His sermon.

Vi's Gardening Tip:

How do you uproot thorns? Certainly not with your bare hands! It takes special, protective gloves and gardening tools to safely and effectively remove these grisly weeds. Thankfully, when dealing with thorns of our heart, our Master Gardener comes to the rescue! Follow these simple guidelines and He will remove those prickly thistles and heal your tattered heart, restoring your joy and strength:

- First, identify the specific thorn(s) in your life and understand how this is harming your spiritual growth.
- Next, talk to your Master Gardener. Tell Him you don't want it there and ask Him to pull it up by the roots. You cannot pull it out yourself, but if you ask Him to do it, He will. Your part in the process is to turn your thoughts back to Jesus.
- Renew your love relationship with Him. Get your eyes back on His goodness and love for you and off of your thorn. You may also need to guard your heart against the temptations that are causing thorns to grow. Commit all worries and cares to Him and trust Him.
- Weeds come out of softened soil easily. Soften your soil by finding a Scripture, such as the passage we listed above, or any promise of God that deals with your particular thorn, and begin to really meditate on it, letting it go deep into the soil of your heart to increase your faith.

- Finally, tending to a garden is not something you do only once; it takes regular attention on your part. Examine your heart regularly before God and He will help you uproot those thorns!

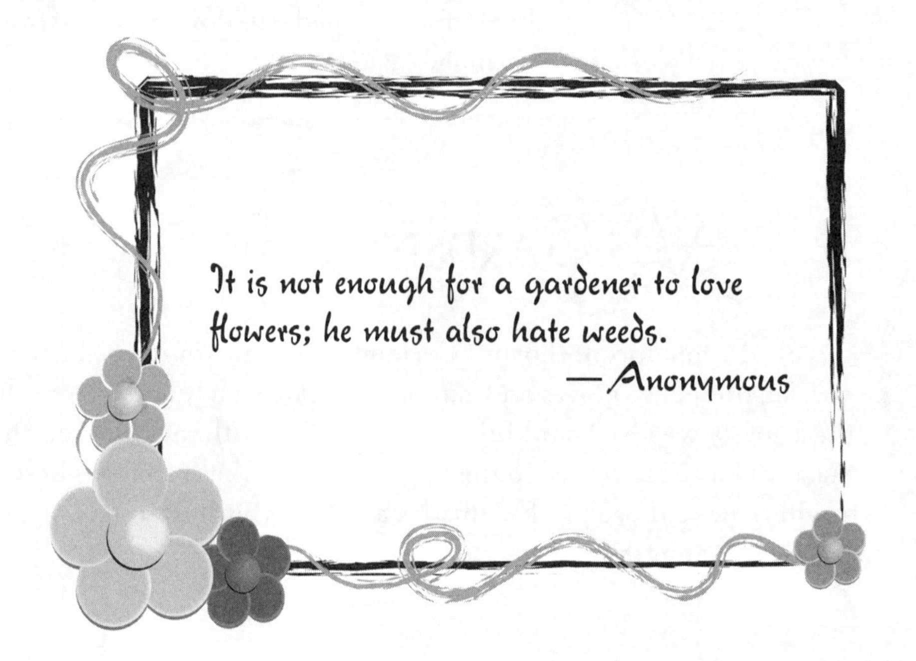

It is not enough for a gardener to love flowers; he must also hate weeds.
—Anonymous

Lesson Seven

Good Ground

There is nothing more beautiful to the gardener than the feel of rich, dark soil trickling through her fingers. It's as precious as gold. Read Matthew 13:8 to learn about this good soil.

> STILL OTHER SEED FELL ON *GOOD SOIL*, WHERE IT PRODUCED A CROP — A HUNDRED, SIXTY OR THIRTY TIMES WHAT WAS SOWN.
>
> — MATTHEW 13:8

How pleased the Master Gardener is to find good soil in a human heart, because He knows the life of His Son can live there and produce a great harvest!

A heart with good ground understands the Word of Truth, believes and receives it, and acts on it with all sincerity and full conviction. Good soil is permeated with humility, faith, and obedience. Such soil is assured a fruitful harvest! Good ground is a soft, tender heart that desires to please the Lord.

Look up Matthew 13:23, write it below, and then reread it carefully to discover what happens to seeds planted in good soil:

Matthew 13:23 speaks of a harvest of a hundred, sixty, or thirty times what was sown. This is the type of soil we want in our hearts as we grow in our lives of faith. This good soil allows the seeds of God's truth to implant, grow, and increase so that there will be a bountiful harvest. Your Master Gardener will bring about the increase for you. Just give Him the garden of your soul—a soft, tender heart with good soil—and watch what wonders He will create from it. Oh, how He enjoys the fruitfulness of such a garden!

Jesus spoke a blessing to those with tender hearts in Matthew 13:16: "Blessed are your eyes because they see, and your ears because they hear." Jesus also spoke a blessing over such open hearts in Matthew 5:6: "Blessed are those who hunger and thirst for righteousness, for they will be filled." In other words, their desire for Him shall be filled. They shall become a harvest of righteousness—bearing fruit: some a hundredfold, some sixty, some thirty.

Let's examine the following passage from 2 Peter 1:3, 5-8 to learn more about the characteristics of good soil in our hearts:

> [3]HIS DIVINE POWER HAS GIVEN US EVERYTHING WE NEED FOR LIFE AND GODLINESS THROUGH OUR KNOWLEDGE OF HIM WHO CALLED US BY HIS OWN GLORY AND GOODNESS.... [5]FOR THIS VERY REASON, MAKE EVERY EFFORT TO ADD TO YOUR FAITH GOODNESS; AND TO GOODNESS, KNOWLEDGE; [6]AND TO KNOWLEDGE, SELF-CONTROL; AND TO SELF-CONTROL, PERSEVERANCE; AND TO PERSEVERANCE, GODLINESS; [7]AND TO GODLINESS, BROTHERLY KINDNESS; AND TO BROTHERLY KINDNESS, LOVE. [8]FOR IF YOU POSSESS THESE QUALITIES IN INCREASING MEASURE, THEY WILL KEEP YOU FROM BEING INEFFECTIVE AND UNPRODUCTIVE IN YOUR KNOWLEDGE OF OUR LORD JESUS CHRIST.
>
> —2 PETER 1:3, 5-8

In the above passage, underline the words "glory" and "goodness." Note that *Christ* is our goodness.

In this passage we see that we can receive Christ's goodness into the soil of our hearts by growing in the knowledge of Christ. In what ways are you growing in the knowledge of Christ and receiving His goodness? Write your thoughts below:

What is the promise that God has given us in 2 Peter 1:3?

Through the life of Christ within us, we have been given everything we need to have good, fertile soil in our hearts. Believe this promise. Notice in the passage above that faith is the foundation for all of the other characteristics that follow.

Next, go back and underline every quality of good soil that you find in the 2 Peter passage. Once you have done this, list the qualities in the left-hand side in the chart on the next page. We'll get you started. Notice that "faith" is the foundational layer. Build up from there. These qualities are like a layering of nutrients and minerals that make the soil of our hearts rich.

Underline the last sentence of the passage—which is a promise of fruitfulness that comes from good soil. A different translation says:

> THE MORE YOU GROW LIKE THIS, THE MORE YOU WILL BECOME PRODUCTIVE AND USEFUL IN YOUR KNOWLEDGE OF OUR LORD JESUS CHRIST. (NEW LIVING TRANSLATION)
>
> —2 PETER 1:8

My Fruitfulness Chart

Goodness	
Faith (The Foundation)	
Qualities of "good soil" found in 2 Peter	Your soil sample

Reflection:

It's time to examine the soil of your heart one last time, measuring your heart against the qualities of "good soil" as outlined in the 2 Peter 1 passage. Rate yourself on each quality you have listed. Do you need to grow in one of these areas? Maybe you are strong in an area. Either way, write down your observations in the "Your soil sample" column. For instance, across from "Faith" you might write "growing in this area." You might observe that you need to improve in the area of "goodness." Note that in the chart across from "Goodness."

Ask your Master Gardener to supply you with more of His power to work this particular nutrient into your soil and to give you faith to believe that He will do it.

Vi's Gardening Tip:

As you can see, a gardener must work diligently to ready the soil for the seed. The dangers—hardened parts of the path, stones, rocks, and thorns—must be removed in order for the plants to grow. Now that you've searched through your heart's garden and removed these obstacles, it is a good idea to walk through your tender garden regularly and guard the soil from being polluted again. If hardened soil, rocks, or thistles begin to appear, quickly call upon the Master Gardener and take care of the problem with Him. Here's a quick list to help you recognize a heart with good soil:

- Remains teachable and humbly receives the Word of God.
- Continues to grow in the knowledge of God.
- Believes the Word and then obeys it.
- Looks honestly within herself, allowing God to reveal areas that need to be changed.
- Quickly repents and turns back to the Lord.
- Hungers to do what is right and to please the Lord.
- Bears good fruit through good works.

But grow in the grace and knowledge of our Lord and Savior Jesus Christ. To him be glory both now and forever! Amen.
—2 Peter 3:18

Lesson Eight

You've done the painstaking and backbreaking work of clearing the ground and readying the soil for planting. You've opened your heart to the Master Gardener, and together, you have softened the hardened footpaths, raked out the stones and rocks, and pulled out the choking thorns and thistles. Along the way, the Master Gardener has taught you how to recognize the characteristics of good soil. Now that your heart has been cultivated, plowed, and turned into rich, fertile soil, it is time to plant the life-giving seeds.

As you hold tiny seeds in your hand, it is hard to imagine that they will transform into good-tasting vegetables, sweet-smelling flowers, or a large, blossoming tree. After all, seeds appear to be nothing more than just insignificant, little particles. How could a bountiful harvest be wrought from such small, simple seeds? But stop and consider the following: *The potential for life is encapsulated in a single seed.* This is a truly powerful and mysterious truth both in the physical world and in our spiritual lives. Indeed, the amazing design and marvel of God is found in a tiny seed!

The process of how a seed grows (germination) is one of God's secret miracles. But the same process happens in your very own life. When God plants a seed of truth within your heart, a fascinating and wondrous process begins. We are watered by the Word of God and new life eventually breaks forth—transforming us! Just as the marvelous germination process is hidden deep within the soil, God begins His "germination" process within the hidden chambers of our hearts. As we grow toward God and live within God's "special conditions," the visible signs of our growth will begin to show as we become more like Christ. Soon, we bear good fruit to share with others.

Whether it's a physical seed or a spiritual seed, both seeds grow in a powerful silence, hidden away from the eyes and the understanding of man. Let's look at the Parable of the Growing Seed found in Mark 4:26-29. In green, draw a picture of a sprout over every reference to the word "seed," including all the stages of its transformation:

> HE ALSO SAID, "THIS IS WHAT THE KINGDOM OF GOD IS LIKE. A MAN SCATTERS SEED ON THE GROUND. NIGHT AND DAY, WHETHER HE SLEEPS OR GETS UP, THE SEED SPROUTS AND GROWS, THOUGH HE DOES NOT KNOW HOW. ALL BY ITSELF THE SOIL PRODUCES GRAIN—FIRST THE STALK, THEN THE HEAD, THEN THE FULL KERNEL IN THE HEAD. AS SOON AS THE GRAIN IS RIPE, HE PUTS THE SICKLE TO IT, BECAUSE THE HARVEST HAS COME."
>
> —MARK 4:26-29

Wheat is grown from a seed (kernel). The seed needs warmth and moisture to allow that outer layer to break away. A shoot and root then emerge, which make up the baby wheat plant. The plant continues to grow where eventually inside the stem, a head of wheat begins to develop. The stem continues to swell until this head emerges at the top. The head contains many seeds that ripen from a soft, milky substance to kernels resembling the one planted. As the head continues to go through the ripening process, it turns from green to gold and then to beige and begins to dry out. When the seeds become very dry and hard, the wheat is then ready to be harvested. This process from germination to harvest takes approximately 3-4 months.

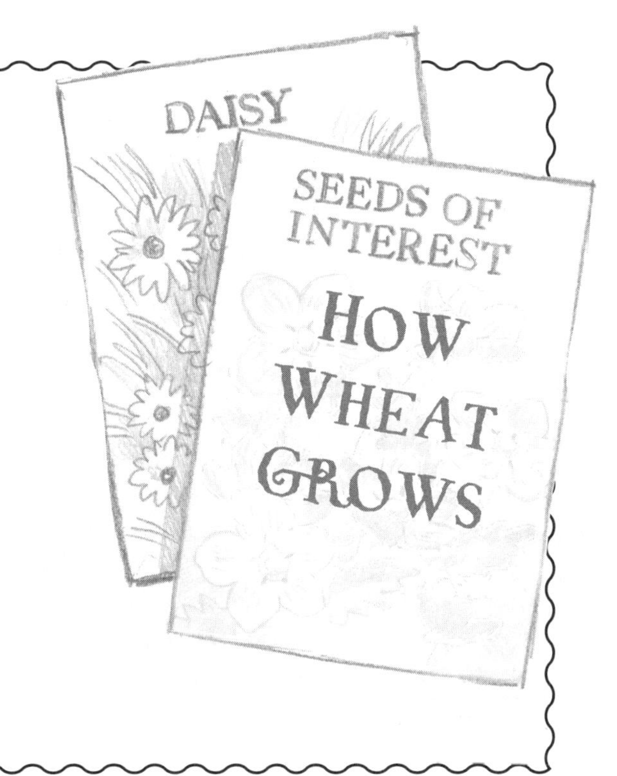

Reflection:

1. From the above passage, list the stages of growth that a grain of wheat goes through from seed to the full kernel.

2. What stage do you think you are at in your spiritual growth? Feel free to expand your description of your stage of growth using the information given in the Seeds of Interest box, such as the sprout, tender shoot, etc. Include your reason for your choice.

Jesus knew that the people He taught would understand the miracle of spiritual growth by comparing it to the growth of a seed. Notice that man plants the seed and then he waits patiently while God causes the seed to grow. It grows secretly, slowly, silently, and purposefully, underground where no eyes can see. Isn't that so in our spiritual lives? So much happens hidden from the human eye. The seed grows stage upon stage under God's care according to His law and design. It is an unseen work and the miraculous transformation comes from within.

The development of Christ's life in you, like this seed, unfolds in stages—slowly, silently, yet powerfully and purposefully accomplishing the good plan that God has for you. Your Master Gardener will cause it to grow until it becomes a mature, ripened plant which then can be harvested. Philippians 1:6 says, "Being confident of this, that he who began a good work in you will carry it on to completion until the day of Christ Jesus."

Just as the man in the parable in Mark 4 trusted God for the growth of the seeds and went peacefully about the tasks of daily life, so you too can trust that God will cause you to grow as you go about your life peacefully day by day. It is His joy and pleasure to do so. He began the work within your heart's garden, and as Philippians 1:6 promises, He will complete it. Your journey of growing toward God will continue throughout your entire life.

The growing process does not happen immediately. Trees don't grow overnight, and neither will we. We must be willing to wait patiently for Christ to bring forth the fruitful harvest of our souls. We can't see the seed beneath the ground beginning to take root and grow. Above ground, all looks the same, dead and barren. But beneath that soil, the miracle of life is coming forth. This is where we must choose to trust our Lord and believe He will do what He promises.

Look up Galatians 6:9 and write it in the space below:

As we water, watch, and wait for new seeds of truth to sprout in our lives, we must not give in to impatience or discouragement. At the proper time we will reap the good seed that has been sown. God determines how long that "proper time" shall be before our seeds produce a harvest. Sometimes, the seeds that we plant will produce a harvest quickly. Other times, we may have to wait years for some of our seeds to produce. In the meantime, we must put our trust in the Lord and not grow weary or impatient. We must stay full of faith and believe God.

What specific "seeds" are you anxiously waiting to see sprout and grow in your own life (for example, growth in the area of patience with a little brother or greater thankfulness for your mom and dad)? List them below:

Vi's Gardening Tip:

God has not forgotten these seeds. He is never early and never late. He is always on time, working what is best for you. Learn from a seasoned farmer, who even though he can't see his seeds growing beneath the soil, knows they are there and that in the right time, a crop will come forth. Trust God with the growing and maturing time for your seeds. Waiting without seeing anything happen is one of the toughest tests of our faith. But as Hebrews 11:1 says, "Faith is being sure of what we hope for and certain of what we do not see."

Though I do not believe that a plant
will spring up where no seed has been, I have great faith in a seed.
Convince me that you have a seed there, and I am prepared to expect wonders.

—Henry David Thoreau

Lesson Nine

Spiritual Seeds

God created a seed to have the power of life within it to grow into a plant, produce fruit, and multiply itself through the seed within the fruit. Read the following verses. Draw a green sprout through every reference to seeds:

> THEN GOD SAID, "LET THE LAND PRODUCE VEGETATION: SEED-BEARING PLANTS AND TREES ON THE LAND THAT BEAR FRUIT WITH SEED IN IT, ACCORDING TO THEIR VARIOUS KINDS." AND IT WAS SO. THE LAND PRODUCED VEGETATION: PLANTS BEARING SEED ACCORDING TO THEIR KINDS AND TREES BEARING FRUIT WITH SEED IN IT ACCORDING TO THEIR KINDS. AND GOD SAW THAT IT WAS GOOD.
>
> —GENESIS 1:11-12

Seeds have been divinely programmed to produce life after themselves. Plants grow from seeds, and their fruit or flowers will release seeds that will make more plants of the same kind. In other words, watermelon seeds will produce watermelons, which will produce watermelon seeds, not beans. Bean seeds will produce beans, etc.

This law of nature, which God has set in motion right from creation, also applies to our spiritual lives. There are such things as spiritual seeds, and the same principles of growth and multiplication apply. Spiritual seeds have the power to grow, to produce some kind of fruit, and to multiply and spread the same seed.

What are some examples of spiritual seeds? Our thoughts, actions, and words are all considered seeds. When sown, they have the power to grow and produce fruit that affects your life and the lives of those around you. Some seeds are good; some are bad. *By observing or inspecting the fruit, you can know what kind of seed has been sown.*

Jesus explains this principle in Matthew 7:15-20. As you read the passage, be sure to mark any words or phrases that seem important:

> WATCH OUT FOR FALSE PROPHETS. THEY COME TO YOU IN SHEEP'S CLOTHING, BUT INWARDLY THEY ARE FEROCIOUS WOLVES. BY THEIR FRUIT YOU WILL RECOGNIZE THEM. DO PEOPLE PICK GRAPES FROM THORNBUSHES, OR FIGS FROM THISTLES? LIKEWISE EVERY GOOD TREE BEARS GOOD FRUIT, BUT A BAD TREE BEARS BAD FRUIT. A GOOD TREE CANNOT BEAR BAD FRUIT, AND A BAD TREE CANNOT BEAR GOOD FRUIT. EVERY TREE THAT DOES NOT BEAR GOOD FRUIT IS CUT DOWN AND THROWN INTO THE FIRE. THUS, BY THEIR FRUIT YOU WILL RECOGNIZE THEM.
>
> —MATTHEW 7:15-20

In your own words, paraphrase Matthew 7:15-20:

How do we know if a seed is good or bad? Become a fruit inspector! "Fruit" is observed by examining or watching outward signs. We need to be aware of the behavior, conduct, and speech of ourselves and other people—not for the sake of judgment but for the sake of wisdom. Remember, fruit is the product of what is planted in the heart, and it affects how people act, what they think, and what they say. Seeds can't be seen once they are planted, but eventually their fruit will be revealed and inspected.

Watch for these three signs:

- How one treats people (Good fruit: respectful and considerate. Bad fruit: demeaning and cruel)
- How one speaks (Good fruit: encouraging and kind. Bad fruit: spiteful and sassy)
- How one behaves (Good fruit: honest and trustworthy. Bad fruit: deceptive and selfish)

Now that we know that spiritual seeds, like natural ones, will grow and produce fruit after their own kind, we can talk about the spiritual principle of sowing and reaping. Let's start by looking at Galatians 6:7-8. Find it in your Bible and write it out below:

In your own words, what is this Scripture saying to you?

This passage gives us a strong warning. As gardeners who are growing toward God, we need to take heed. Verse 7 says, "Do not be deceived: God cannot be mocked." Another way to say it would be, "Do not be fooled or conned. God cannot be insulted, laughed at, or ridiculed." God does not want His children to be deceived into thinking that they can get away with bad behavior without eventually suffering negative consequences. Bad seeds will produce bad fruit, just as good seeds will produce good fruit. God will not be mocked. His laws cannot be changed. You may not see consequences of bad seeds immediately, but they will eventually come.

Now let's define what it means to sow and reap. To "sow" means to scatter for the purpose of a crop, to spread, to plant, or to produce. "Reap" means to receive the fruit of your labor, to gather in, to collect the crop. *Whether we know it or not, we are all spiritual farmers who constantly sow and reap.* We each sow various sorts of seed and we will each reap the results of those seeds planted. It is important to know that the results of the seeds you sow not only affect your life, but also the lives of those around you.

So how does this work? Remember we said that our thoughts, words, actions, and choices are all "seeds" that we sow in life. The consequences (or results) of the seeds that are sown are what one reaps. Reaping can be in the form of rewards or negative consequences, depending on the seed sown.

Here are some practical examples to illustrate the principle of sowing and reaping:

If you sow seeds of kindness by helping your little brother with his math homework, you will reap a closer relationship with your brother. By receiving your help and kindness (the good seed) he reaps by getting a good grade in math. It's a "win-win" situation. Here's another example of sowing and reaping: If you sow seeds of impatience by yelling at your little brother when he asks for your help, it will not only hurt his feelings, but you will reap disharmony between you and your brother, as well as create tension in your home.

Sowing according to God's Spirit is thinking, believing, and acting according to the truth of God's Word—allowing the life of Christ to rule and reign in and through you. This type of sowing is assured to produce a good harvest (or crop) in your life and in the lives of those around you. Let's look closely at what this good fruit looks like. Look up Galatians 5:22-23 and write it below:

This is the fruit that is produced in our garden through the life of Christ growing in us. What a delightful and pleasing crop to offer to your Master Gardener and to others!

Now, get out your nose plugs and let's look at the putrid, rotten, and poisonous fruit that comes from sowing or planting bad seeds, which the Bible calls sowing by "the sinful nature" (also called "the flesh").

> THE ACTS OF THE SINFUL NATURE ARE OBVIOUS: SEXUAL IMMORALITY, IMPURITY AND DEBAUCHERY; IDOLATRY AND WITCHCRAFT; HATRED, DISCORD, JEALOUSY, FITS OF RAGE, SELFISH AMBITION, DISSENSIONS, FACTIONS AND ENVY; DRUNKENNESS, ORGIES, AND THE LIKE. I WARN YOU, AS I DID BEFORE, THAT THOSE WHO LIVE LIKE THIS WILL NOT INHERIT THE KINGDOM OF GOD.
>
> —GALATIANS 5:19-21

If you do not know the meanings of some of these words, ask an adult to go over them with you one at a time. As children of God, we need to be informed of the pitfalls that will lead us into sin. Note the warning in the last verse for those who live this kind of lifestyle! Write it below:

Eating of this poisonous fruit produces corruption to the reaper and to those connected to the reaper. *Corruption* is defined as the state of being putrid—a foul state, like rotten, decaying fruit. How would you enjoy eating from a bowl of rotten, decaying fruit? Even worse, would you want to offer this kind of fruit to Jesus? He desires the fruit that comes from our lives to be good fruit.

REFLECTION:

Now it's time to do some self-examination. What type of seeds are you sowing? Are you sowing seeds "according to the Spirit" or "according to the flesh"? Look at the fruit of your life for the answer.

First let's look to see if there is any rotten fruit in your life. Are you easily angered? Do you pick fights with your siblings? Are you selfish? Do you feel jealous or envious at times? Do you gossip or say mean things about people? Determine if there is rotten fruit in your heart's garden. Write your thoughts below:

Now let's look for the good fruit. Can you see the fruit of the Spirit of Christ growing in your life? Go back to the list of the fruit of the Spirit and put "I am" in front of each quality: I am loving. I am joyful. I am peaceable, etc. Is this you? Write below the good fruit you see growing in your garden:

The principle of sowing and reaping is one that we must learn as we grow in Christ. It applies to our personal gardens, but also affects our work in the harvest that we will discuss later. There will be an ultimate reaping which will come on that glorious day when Christ returns. We will discuss this more in our Final Harvest lesson at the end of the study guide.

When you look inside your heart, if you find rotten fruit, don't despair. We all have to struggle with our sinful nature. Go back to our discussion on footpaths and repentance. Your Master Gardener will help you tend your garden so that it will grow luscious, good fruit. There is so much hope for us because of Christ. Keep going in our study and you will discover the secret of bearing good fruit through Christ.

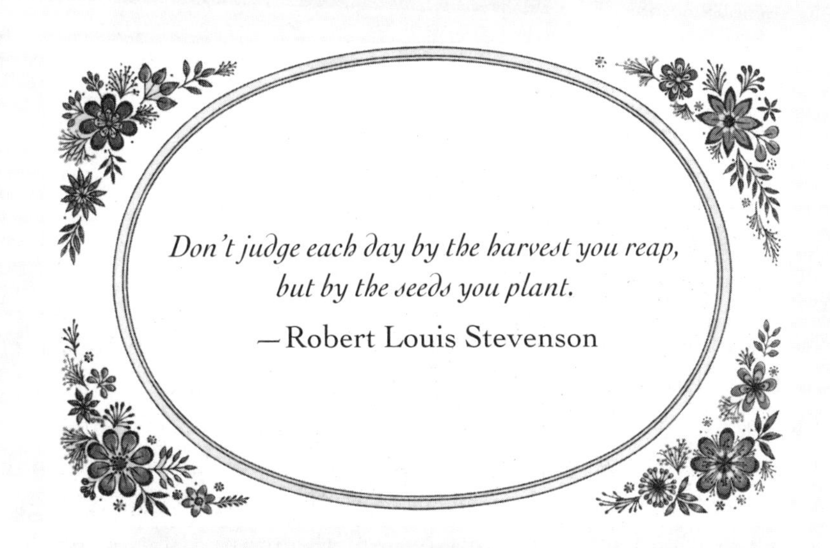

Don't judge each day by the harvest you reap,
but by the seeds you plant.
—Robert Louis Stevenson

Lesson Ten

The Snake in Your Garden

We learned earlier that we each have a responsibility to watch over our gardens. In ancient Israel, a watchtower was erected in the middle of a garden or vineyard. A watchman was stationed in it day and night to guard the precious crop against enemies, such as wild animals or thieves. You must also keep a vigilant watch day and night over the garden of your heart because there is an enemy who wants to destroy your love relationship (your communion) with God. This enemy is trying to sow bad seeds in your garden. Beware of him. He is subtle, seductive, and very deceptive. He slithers and slinks under rocks or logs and waits for an opportune time to plant bad seeds, usually in your thoughts. If left unchecked, bad thoughts will produce bad behavior (sin), and this is the enemy's strategy. He wants to lure you to sin. Sin separates us from God, and this is what the snake is after. This serpent is none other than God's archenemy and yours, Satan.

After God cursed Satan in the Garden of Eden, Satan was reduced to crawling on his belly, thus we call him a snake. And a snake he is. He loves to strike when you are weak and vulnerable, and he will disguise himself to look innocent and good so you won't recognize him. Let's look closely at how this crafty serpent spoke to Eve so we can learn how to recognize him when he speaks to us in our thoughts.

Underline everything Satan says in black. Underline what Eve says in green.

> [1]NOW THE SERPENT WAS MORE CRAFTY THAN ANY OF THE WILD ANIMALS THE LORD GOD HAD MADE. HE SAID TO THE WOMAN, "DID GOD REALLY SAY, 'YOU MUST NOT EAT FROM ANY TREE IN THE GARDEN'?"
>
> [2]THE WOMAN SAID TO THE SERPENT, "WE MAY EAT FRUIT FROM THE TREES IN THE GARDEN, [3]BUT GOD DID SAY, 'YOU MUST NOT EAT FRUIT FROM THE TREE THAT IS IN THE MIDDLE OF THE GARDEN, AND YOU MUST NOT TOUCH IT, OR YOU WILL DIE.' "
>
> [4]"YOU WILL NOT SURELY DIE," THE SERPENT SAID TO THE WOMAN. [5]"FOR GOD KNOWS THAT WHEN YOU EAT OF IT YOUR EYES WILL BE OPENED, AND YOU WILL BE LIKE GOD, KNOWING GOOD AND EVIL." [6]WHEN THE WOMAN SAW THAT THE FRUIT OF THE TREE WAS GOOD FOR FOOD AND PLEASING TO THE EYE, AND ALSO DESIRABLE FOR GAINING WISDOM, SHE TOOK SOME AND ATE IT. SHE ALSO GAVE SOME TO HER HUSBAND, WHO WAS WITH HER, AND HE ATE IT.
>
> —GENESIS 3:1-6

Satan has been using the same weapons since the beginning of time and we can learn to recognize him when he speaks to us. As in any battle, we must know who our enemy is and how he behaves so we do not fall prey to his wicked schemes. Here are three ways Satan will try to deceive you:

1. He will try to get you to believe that disobeying God is not really a sin and that God and His Word are not good and true. Fill in Satan's quote from verse 1:

____

2. He will lie and tell you that nothing bad will happen if you sin or that there will be no negative consequences for your sins. Fill in Satan's quote found in verse 4:

____

3. He will try to emphasize the good or the advantage of the sinful behavior, making it look pleasant in your eyes. He will try to deceive you into believing that you are "missing out" or that God is withholding something from you. Fill in Satan's quote from verse 5:

____

You can and should take safeguards to protect yourself from Satan. Here are some ways you can protect yourself from the schemes of the devil:

1. Do not listen to or try to argue with the deceptive lies of Satan. He is craftier than you. Do not entertain temptation or bad thoughts. Nip them off at the bud! The more you dwell on negative or bad thoughts, the stronger and more powerful they become, and the harder it is to stand against them. The more Eve looked at the apple and listened to the serpent, the weaker she became until she finally ate—disobeying God. Look up James 4:7 and write it below:

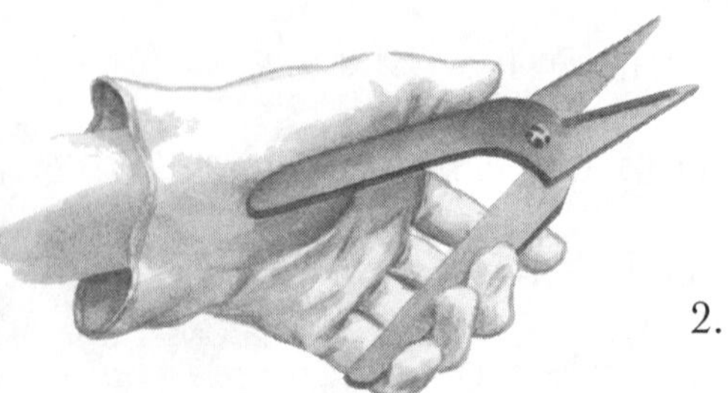

2. Bad seeds can be formed in our minds by what we allow our minds to dwell on. We must be aware of what music we listen to, what we watch on TV, and what material we read. Replace negative thinking with God's Word.

Look at Philippians 4:8 for a list of what our minds should think about. Let these be seeds of truth for your thought life. Draw a flower around each of the seed types that you should be planting in your thoughts.

> FINALLY, BROTHERS, WHATEVER IS TRUE, WHATEVER IS NOBLE, WHATEVER IS RIGHT, WHATEVER IS PURE, WHATEVER IS LOVELY, WHATEVER IS ADMIRABLE—IF ANYTHING IS EXCELLENT OR PRAISEWORTHY—THINK ABOUT SUCH THINGS.
>
> —PHILIPPIANS 4:8

Think about what you are thinking about. Make your thoughts line up with God's Word. Be very aggressive with this. It's easy to be passive and let any old thought take over. Beware! What you are thinking directly affects how you feel (your emotions) and how you act (your behavior). Look up 2 Corinthians 10:5 and write it below:

Underline the military terminology in this passage. Notice the aggressive action we are to take against such thoughts. In your own words, explain what it means to take your thoughts "captive."

REFLECTION:

What is your thought life like? Use the seeds of truth from Philippians 4:8 as a guide to examine your thoughts. Do you struggle with impure thoughts (secretly hoping a friend loses an audition), negative thinking (telling yourself that you'll *never* be as smart as your big sister), or fearful thoughts (consuming anxiety about getting a terminal illness)? Take a few minutes to ask your Master Gardener to help you examine your thoughts, and write what He reveals to you below:

Now apply 2 Corinthians 10:5 to your thought life!

- Know what is true. Make it your daily assignment to know what God's Word says; these are your seeds of truth. God's truths will help you recognize the lies that Satan will try to get you to believe. Fear, anxiety, depression, and other negative feelings are often symptoms of having believed a lie. Find the lie of Satan behind these feelings (such as, "I am afraid God does not love me"). Replace the lie with the truth in God's Word (such as, "John 3:16 assures me that God does love me!"). Satan is so crafty that sometimes the lie itself is not so obvious. You may be battling a vague feeling of not seeming as special or valuable as those around you. Sometimes you may need to ask God to reveal the lie.
- Stay connected in fellowship with others. Be honest and open with a trustworthy adult mentor about your particular struggles. Ask your mentor to pray that you will resist the lies of the devil. List at least one adult you can trust to give you godly support:

  ____
- Never focus on Satan, the snake. When you are being tempted, immediately look into the face of your Master Gardener and ask for help. Begin to recite a Scripture (as Jesus did when He was tempted in the wilderness in Matthew 4), or sing a worship song. Choose one Scripture from the Seed Packets of Truth cards in the back of this book that you can memorize and recite when you feel tempted. Write it here: ______________

Vi's Gardening Tip:

Never underestimate the power of your thoughts. Your thought life is a wide-open field where seeds, good or bad, can take root. It's up to you to decide which seeds are going to grow there. Remember, as your thoughts take root and grow, they will produce an effect in your emotions and your behavior. There's that sowing and reaping principle again! Be a very diligent watchman when it comes to your thought life.

Your mind is a garden, your thoughts are the seeds,
the harvest can be either flowers or weeds.

—Author Unknown

Lesson Eleven

The Seed of God

There are many, many thousands of types of seeds in the natural world, and as we have learned, each seed is uniquely designed to bring forth life according to its kind. In other words, you don't plant a watermelon and reap a bean plant. Nor does God plant a seed of faith within us only for doubt to spring forth. But there is *one* Seed in the universe that stands above all the rest. This particular Seed is more powerful than the deceptive seeds that the snake tries to sow into our lives. This Seed is the greatest, most powerful, and most precious Seed of all; the only Seed that can bring forth spiritual life. Take a guess as to who or what is this spiritual Seed:

____

Now let's dig into the rich soil of God's Word and unfold this little mystery to discover more about this Supernatural Seed. Read the following passage of Scripture taken from the Amplified Bible. (You will notice that the Amplified translation contains brackets and parentheses. These are for the purpose of giving you more clarification and understanding into the verses.) Underline the word "curse" in red. Make a pink star around the words "blessing" and "promise":

> [13]CHRIST PURCHASED OUR FREEDOM [REDEEMING US] FROM THE CURSE (DOOM) OF THE LAW [AND ITS CONDEMNATION] BY [HIMSELF] BECOMING A CURSE FOR US, FOR IT IS WRITTEN [IN THE SCRIPTURES], CURSED IS

everyone who hangs on a tree (is crucified). [14]To the end that through [their receiving] Christ Jesus, the blessing [promised] to Abraham might come upon the Gentiles, so that we through faith might [all] receive [the realization of] the promise of the [Holy] Spirit.... [16]Now the promises (covenants, agreements) were decreed and made to Abraham and his Seed (his Offspring, his Heir). He [God] does not say, And to seeds (descendants, heirs), as if referring to many persons, but, And to your Seed (your Descendant, your Heir), obviously referring to one individual, Who is [none other than] Christ (the Messiah).

—Galatians 3:13-14, 16 (Amplified)

How did Jesus free us from the curse of the law? (verse 13)

How do we receive the promise of the Holy Spirit and the blessing of life in Christ? (verse 14)

Who is this Seed mentioned in verse 16 to whom the promises were made and fulfilled?

The word "seed" also means descendant, son, or heir. Whom is Christ a descendant of?

Jesus took the curse of punishment for our sins and our inability to keep God's holy laws and put them to death with Himself on the Cross. The Cross is also called a "tree" since it was made of wood. Deuteronomy 21:22-23 says that those who are hung on a tree to die are cursed of God. When He died on the Cross, Jesus became our curse. We no longer have to try to please God through obeying the law or a system of commands. Abraham is called the Father of Faith because he believed in God's promises. Because Abraham believed, he was considered "righteous" (i.e., virtuous, commendable, "right" with God). We, too, like Abraham, receive the promise of God through putting our faith in Christ, who is the descendant of Abraham and the Son of God. What is the promise that we receive? It is that God's Holy Spirit will live in us and through us, making us holy, pleasing, and right with the Father. Jesus is God's Seed — God's Son. His life, implanted and living in us, also makes us children of God.

Let's look more closely at what it means to have Christ, the Seed, implanted in our hearts. In our previous lesson we learned that God has programmed seeds to produce after their own kind (tomatoes don't produce broccoli; they produce tomatoes!). If Jesus is truly the life-giving, spiritual Seed of God, and if He is implanted deep within our hearts, then something magnificent will happen — He will produce a harvest of Christlikeness within us. In practical terms, what does this look like? Well, instead of feeling jealous or hateful toward someone, the seed of Christ within us changes us into people who can be happy for others and live in peace with people. Instead of being fearful and timid, we become confident in the Lord. Rather than being overcome with worry, we are filled with joyful expectancy of what God can do in any given situation.

What an awesome thing — Jesus, the Seed of God, rooted and growing in the good soil of our hearts, bringing forth good fruit! Just think of all the wonderful character traits of Jesus Christ, and now imagine those same attributes growing in *you*! Jesus' new life in us is a miracle-working power that transforms our very lives!

Let's apply this practical application to your own life.

Reflection:

List three different weaknesses that you struggle with. Then, in the opposite column, write how the life of Jesus growing in you can produce good fruit:

I struggle with . . .	**Jesus' life in me . . .**
Jealousy	Helps me be happy for people who have things that I want.
Fear of Harm	Assures me that God is watching over me.

Now review your chart. You see, you *really can change* with Christ growing in you. He makes you into something new. Second Corinthians 12:9 says that His strength is perfected (made complete) in your areas of weakness. The best part of all, and a very important fact to remember, is that it's not up to us to produce the life of Jesus in our lives. We need only to open our hearts to Him and make sure that we are obeying His Word and resting in His care over us, and *He* will bring forth His life, His righteousness, and all that He is into our lives.

To clarify this point, think again about the seed. When the soil is prepared just right, the seed is planted by the hands of God, our Master Gardener. He waters it and sees that the conditions for growth are just right. The seed simply allows itself to be planted, and mysteriously, it grows without any fussing, striving, or toiling of its own. It does only what it was intended to do—grow and produce fruit. What freedom for the believer in Christ! What joy to be in the hands of the Master Gardener! We cannot make ourselves become like Jesus. But we can ask Jesus to have His way in our lives, and when we do, He grows and blossoms and blooms within us. This life in Christ is more precious than any earthly possession, position, or promotion. Life in Christ is where true living is really at!

Vi's Gardening Tip:

Have you really grasped hold of this unbelievable life God offers you? Can you see how Jesus is like an everlasting, imperishable seed that changes your life and transforms you into something so amazing—a reflection of Himself? What *can't* you do with Christ growing within you? What fear *can't* you face? What struggle *can't* you overcome? Be assured that you can do everything through Him (Christ) who gives you strength! (Philippians 4:13). Give thanks to God, your Master Gardener, for the life of Christ He is growing within you!

There is a little plant called reverence in the corner of my soul's garden, which I love to have watered once a week.

—Oliver Wendell Holmes

JESUS AND GARDENS

In the Bible there are many fascinating verses in which Jesus is referred to as or compared to different garden-themed terms, such as a vine or a branch. We've featured some below. Read through the following list and delight in Jesus, the Seed of God!

- **Jesus was with God in the Garden of Eden**: "He was with God in the beginning." (John 1:2)
- **Jesus as a seed**: "The promises were spoken to Abraham and to his seed. The Scripture does not say 'and to seeds,' meaning many people, but 'and to your seed,' meaning one person, who is Christ." (Galatians 3:16)
- **Jesus as a tender shoot**: "He grew up before him like a tender shoot, and like a root out of dry ground." (Isaiah 53:2)
- **Jesus as a vine**: "I am the vine; you are the branches. If a man remains in me and I in him, he will bear much fruit; apart from me you can do nothing." (John 15:5)
- **Jesus as a branch**: "A shoot will come up from the stump of Jesse; from his roots a Branch will bear fruit." (Isaiah 11:1)
- **Jesus prayed in a garden called Gethsemane**: "Then Jesus went with his disciples to a place called Gethsemane, and he said to them, 'Sit here while I go over there and pray.' " (Matthew 26:36)
- **Jesus hung on a cross, which is often referred to as a "tree"**: "But Christ has rescued us from the curse pronounced by the law. When he was hung on the cross, he took upon himself the curse for our wrongdoing. For it is written in the Scriptures, 'Cursed is everyone who is hung on a tree.'" (Galatians 3:13, NLT)
- **Jesus was buried in a garden tomb**: "At the place where Jesus was crucified, there was a garden, and in the garden a new tomb, in which no one had ever been laid." (John 19:41)
- **Jesus was mistaken for a gardener by Mary Magdalene at the garden tomb**: "At this, she turned around and saw Jesus standing there, but she did not realize that it was Jesus. 'Woman,' he said, 'why are you crying? Who is it you are looking for?' Thinking he was the gardener, she said, 'Sir, if you have carried him away, tell me where you have put him, and I will get him.' " (John 20:14-15)
- **Jesus as the firstfruits**: "But Christ has indeed been raised from the dead, the firstfruits of those who have fallen asleep." (1 Corinthians 15:20)

A ROSE STORY

ONCE UPON A TIME there was a perfect rose garden. Living in it was a bed of special, perfect roses; roses with no thorns, that is. The Master Gardener loved His rose garden and His two prized rose "plants"—named Adam and Eve. Everyone was happy in the garden and life was rosy. But one day a snake slithered in and tempted Adam and Eve to disobey the Master Gardener. Because of this act of disobedience, sin entered in and immediately a curse was set in motion—the curse of the thorns and thistles. Adam and Eve were uprooted and cast from the perfect rose garden into an imperfect world. They didn't look like roses anymore. Instead, they became thistle plants.

Now, when they worked in their gardens, it was hard and toilsome labor. They had to fight the wild thistles and thorns and a lot of other bad stuff [(1)]. This went on for a long time. Many generations of thistles were born, and they forgot about God and what was right. So God gave them the Law, the Ten Commandments, to remind them of what was right. But the curse of the thorns and thistles still continued because the commandments could not break the curse and make them into roses again.

When the time was right, God sent His Son, the Rose of Sharon [(2)], to live among the thistles and teach them about God's love for them. Many of the thistles believed in the Rose of Sharon, but others did not and became angry at Him. They wove a crown of thorns and put it on His head. They beat Him with thorny whips and then nailed Him to a tree to die. The Rose of Sharon shed His precious red petals on the Cross to cover the sins of all the thistles—past, present, and future. They buried Him in a garden tomb. But like a seed planted in the ground, the Rose of Sharon burst forth into glorious life and was raised up as the most radiant Rose of all!

From that point on, whenever the thistles believed in the Rose of Sharon, He came and planted His holy seed in their hearts. Then, the most wonderful, powerful thing began to happen. The seed of the Rose of Sharon slowly transformed the thistles into roses [(3)]. Gradually over time, the thistles looked more and more like the Rose of Sharon. But, alas, they still had one thing that they couldn't get rid of—the thorns. They became roses with thorns because they were still living in a world of sin that was under the curse of thorns and thistles. Their bodies were still weak and susceptible to sin.

The thorns worried the new rose plants and became a real "thorn in their flesh", but the Rose of Sharon assured them that He would use the thorns for a good purpose. Through the weakness caused by their thorns, they would learn to trust in and lean on the Rose of Sharon and He would be strong in them [(4)]. The Rose of Sharon also encouraged His new roses to see themselves as roses, not what they used to be—thistles. They were released from the curse of thorns and thistles, even though for a short time they had to live with thorns. He wanted them to live and bloom and release the fragrance of the new life growing in them so that other thistles would also see and believe and be changed into roses [(5)].

The Rose of Sharon gave them a promise that one day they would once again be made into perfect roses with no thorns. One day He would come and harvest His roses and gather them into the most fragrant, beautiful bouquet the world has ever known. He will wipe every tear from their eyes and take all their thorns away. And they will live forever in the new rose garden with the Rose of Sharon and the Master Gardener in joy and gladness [(6)].

1. Genesis 3:17-18 / 2. Song of Songs 2:1 / 3. 2 Corinthians 3:18 / 4. 2 Corinthians 12:7-8 /
5. 2 Corinthians 2:14-15 / 6. Revelation 21:1-4

Lesson Twelve

Working in Your Garden

Pause for a moment and think about how far you've come in our study of the heart's garden. Already you have learned so much about cultivating your spiritual growth. The truths you are embracing are tools that you can use for the rest of your life. God's precepts are timeless! Now that you've readied the flower beds and planted the precious spiritual seeds, let's look at some ways you can nurture your fledgling garden to ensure that the seeds will grow strong and healthy.

As we learned, water is a key factor in starting the germination process. Once water is absorbed into the dry seed, a chemical reaction starts the growth process. The same is true for our spiritual lives. We need to water the seeds that Christ plants deep into our hearts. Today we will look at some ways you can "water those seeds."

Look up 1 Thessalonians 5:16-18 and write it below. We will refer to it throughout today's lesson:

One way to water our garden is through the Word of God. A thorough and careful study of God's Word is like a nice gentle shower on the soil of our hearts. Learn to read the Bible to receive something from the Lord. *When you approach the Scriptures, keep in mind that you are reading to get heart transformation, not heady information.* This approach may require you to do some nice, slow grazing, like a cow. Have you ever seen a cow graze? She will take a bite of grass and then she will chew it and chew it and chew it. This is called "chewing the cud" and it allows for slow, thorough digestion. Sounds crazy, but this is how we should approach God's Word.

Try reading a small passage of Scripture and then go back over the passage again. Pray, asking the Lord to speak to you through His Word. Think about the concept the passage is relaying. Include Bible memorization in your study so you can further ponder the truths of God's Word and call forth that particular verse whenever you need it. Hiding God's Word in your heart is a special treasure that will encourage you in times of weakness or trouble. Hebrews 4:12 says that God's Word is living and active—let the Word have its way in your heart.

Let's put this into practice. Look again at the 1 Thessalonians passage. Re-read the verses several times. Think about what it is saying. Ask the Lord to speak to you—take a few minutes to "chew the cud," so to speak. Write any insights or impressions below:

Another method of watering the seeds in your heart is through prayer—and lots of it! What does 1 Thessalonians 5:17 say about how we should pray?

How is this possible, you may wonder? Actually, praying without ceasing keeps prayer simple. It is merely talking with God all day long in your thoughts. If Christ lives in you, then your "prayer-line" is connected to Him all the time. Praying helps you remember that you're not alone; you can always talk to God, who cares for you and hears you. For more great ideas to help enliven your prayer life, read *Millie's Prayer Projects: Fun and Creative Ways to Pray* by Mission City Press.

You don't have to pray in ritual forms, such as using a certain posture or praying at a specific time. You can do these things if you want to, but the beauty of your relationship with Christ is that you can talk to Him all throughout your day in whatever way is natural for you. Remember, you can go to your garden of communion with God anytime you want. He is always there waiting for you!

Reflection:

1. Think about your prayer life for a moment. How often do you pray? When do you pray? Where do you pray? Answer these three questions in the space below:

2. Review your answers. How can you make prayer more a part of your life? Write your thoughts below:

We've looked at God's Word and prayer as two important means of watering the soil of our hearts. Now let's look at some fun ways we can add nutrients and minerals to feed the soil. Look again at 1 Thessalonians 5:16. What else does it say to do? Write your answer below:

You can add rich fertilizer to invigorate your growth through praise and worship. Cultivating an attitude of joy is good for us! How do we do this? *Praise* expresses jubilant gratitude and thankfulness toward God (see verse 18). *Worship* is reverently honoring and adoring God. Praise and worship will give you a good spiritual adjustment. Praise can be the cure for stress, anxiety, or fear. It keeps us in an attitude of gratitude. It's a great cure for those pesky garden weeds. When we worship God for who He is and thank Him for what He does, we suddenly take our eyes off of ourselves and our problems and realize how big and able God is to take care of us. Praise and worship restores our joy.

Next, look up Hebrews 10:24-25 and write it below:

In addition to praise and worship, fellowshipping with other Christians is another great way to keep the soil of your heart rich and fertile. We receive tremendous encouragement, support, and protection when we gather with other believers to worship, pray, care for one another, and share in God's Word together. We need one another in our journey of faith.

Sharing your faith with others is one last tip to help keep your garden healthy and fresh. Of course, that's what this study is all about—growing in God and then sharing the "fruits" of your personal harvest with others in the "Great Harvest." For more of Vi's practical advice for sharing your faith with others, refer to the book *Dear Violet: Advice for the Harvest* from Mission City Press.

There is no greater joy than watching God take a broken, hopeless soul and restore it to hope and life. And no greater reward is there in this life than knowing that God has used you in the process.

List the different ways we've discussed in this lesson on how to fertilize and water your seeds:

Vi's Gardening Tip:

Miracle Grow® is a popular, specialized fertilizer that many gardeners "feed" to their plants to help them grow stronger and healthier. As Christians, we have our own "miracle grow"—God's Word! The following promises found in Isaiah 55:9-11 are precious to us as we conclude today's lesson. Allow these comforting words to put to rest any doubt that God can and will cause His seeds of truth to take root and grow in your heart. Encourage yourself with this passage when you feel discouraged. "Feeding" on the Scriptures will cause your faith to grow strong!

> As the heavens are higher than the earth, so are my ways higher than your ways and my thoughts than your thoughts. As the rain and the snow come down from heaven, and do not return to it without watering the earth and making it bud and flourish, so that it yields seed for the sower and bread for the eater, so is my word that goes out from my mouth: It will not return to me empty, but will accomplish what I desire and achieve the purpose for which I sent it.
>
> — Isaiah 55:9-11

Opportunity is missed by most people because it is dressed in overalls and looks like work.
—Thomas A. Edison

Lesson Thirteen

Now that we've got the tools to work effectively in the gardens of our hearts and grow healthy, strong seeds, let's look closely at exactly how a seed becomes life—a fascinating process called *germination,* which so wonderfully demonstrates the thrilling wisdom of God.

After a wrinkled, dry seed is planted in fertile soil, an abundance of water must be absorbed by the seed to get the germination process started. When the seed is saturated in water, it activates an enzyme, respiration thus increases, and plant cells begin to duplicate. Soon, a tiny seedling begins to emerge from the seed. The embryo continues to grow larger until the seed coat bursts open and eventually falls off—*the seed completely loses its original identity as the new, transformed life appears!* The seed "gives up" itself for the embryo. If the seed coat remains stubbornly intact, the new developing life within will never come forth.

Most seeds need special conditions in order to germinate effectively, such as good soil, the proper amount of water/moisture and light, and correct temperatures. Think about your own spiritual growth. What "special conditions" will help maximize your spiritual growth? (Hint: We have learned about several so far in this study guide, such as avoiding thorns.) Write some below:

It may seem strange that the life of a seed is brought forth through death, but it's true. This is a wondrous, vital truth in our spiritual lives, too. First Corinthians 15:36 reiterates this seed secret. It says, "What you sow does not come to life unless it dies." Jesus refers to this concept in John 12:24-25. Look up these verses and write them below:

The seed (kernel of wheat) mentioned in verse 24 must go through a death for the wheat to be produced. If the seed dies, look at the multiplication that happens—many seeds come forth! Note that the head on the stalk of wheat has many seeds in it, just as we learned in Lesson 8—Seeds.

In verse 25, Jesus says that the man who "hates" his life in this world will gain eternal life. In simpler terms, this concept is about a death to our own will—also known as "dying to our will" or "death to self." Our "will" is our ability to declare our own choices or to determine our own actions. We can use our "will" for good or for bad.

Christ, our Heavenly Seed, modeled this concept of "dying to our will" (or forsaking the things of this world) when He faced death on the Cross. Jesus prayed, "Father, if you are willing, take this cup from me; yet not my will, but yours be done" (Luke 22:42). Jesus set aside His own desire to forgo a brutal death on behalf of sinners. This was the will of God the Father.

Jesus submitted His heart, His body, and His will to God. He died a physical death and was buried in a tomb (a *garden* tomb!). But Jesus received an invaluable blessing from His sacrifice and obedience, for three days later, God performed a miracle and raised Jesus from the dead! Jesus was lifted into the Heavens and is now seated at the right hand of God! Not only did Jesus receive a blessing for His sacrifice, but all who call on Jesus as Lord and Savior receive the priceless blessing of eternal life. But before all of this could happen, Jesus had to die. He came to a crossroads and made a choice between His own will and wants and those of His Father.

As Christians, we may find ourselves saying a similar prayer to Jesus: "Dear Lord, I really don't want to give up ________________, but if it pleases You, I will do it."

It is not always easy to give up our "rights" in order to please God—like avoiding listening to inappropriate music groups or viewing certain movies. Bowing our will to God is a sacrifice, just as it was for Jesus. But the sacrifice will bring blessings into our lives. God always directs us into areas that are for our benefit, not to make us feel like we are missing out or being deprived of something.

Sometimes our will may become stubborn—times when we absolutely do not want to bend to God's ways. The outer coating of a seed can represent a stubborn will. Jeremiah 7:24 says, "But they did not listen or pay attention; instead, they followed the stubborn inclinations of their evil hearts. They went backward and not forward."

Whenever our will is contrary to God's will, we can hinder the spiritual life of Christ within us. In these cases, Christ, the embryo of new life, remains locked inside of our hard seed coat and cannot be released to grow and bloom. When our will does not agree with God's will, we face a crossroad just as Jesus did. In those times, we can't have both. One must die. We must choose between life and death. In order to choose life, we first must choose death—death to ourselves by giving up our stubborn will in favor of God's will.

Reflection:

Do you sometimes find yourself in a struggle with your will? You sense God's truth tugging at your heart, yet you want to go your "own way." This is a common conflict that all Christians face throughout their spiritual growth. Learning to identify our selfish patterns and then facing them with God's Word and Holy Spirit is the certain path to victory.

Recount a *specific* situation that you can remember when you battled against your will and write it down below. (Example: *"I was at school when some friends started gossiping about a new girl. I joined in, but a part of me knew that it was wrong . . . but, I didn't want to stop. My 'flesh' wanted to do it, but in my heart I knew it was wrong."*)

Of course, "death to self" is a process. We don't just decide once and for all that we're going to "die" to ourselves. We have to choose daily. Turn to Colossians 3:5 and write out the verse below:

We have the Spirit of God through the seed of Christ growing in us, helping us to overcome our sinful desires. When we say "No" to our sinful nature—"No" to that hard seed coating—we allow for the precious, tender shoot of Christ's life to come forth. As an encouragement, look up Titus 2:11-14 and write it below. Consider memorizing this verse and referring to it when you are in a struggle with your will.

The following list contains some common struggles regarding our human will or sin nature (the hard seed coat). Review the list and search your heart. What areas in your life might be hindering the growth of Christ? In other words, in what areas is your "original" seed coating still strong and intact? Circle problem areas that you can identify, or write down a struggle if one is not listed here.

Overeating	Too much TV	Laziness
Anger	Cheating	Lying
Impurity	Complacency	Selfishness
Perfectionism	Worrying	Gossip
Fear	Hateful thoughts	Jealousy
Haughtiness	Critical of self	Mouthiness
Bossiness	Mean-Spiritedness	Rebellion
Rudeness		

Why do you think these particular struggles are so hard for you? Write your thoughts below: (Example: *"If I'm honest, when I gossip about others it makes me feel better about myself."*)

What is one simple change you can make this week that will help you overcome these struggles?

Vi's Gardening Tip:

The moment God's Holy Spirit first alerts us to choosing a right path over a wrong one (His will over our will) is the moment we need to be decisive and choose the ways of God. If we linger and debate within our minds (remember our lesson on the snake), chances are we will choose what the "flesh" wants and reject God's best for our lives. Practice responding *immediately* to those promptings and soon that area of struggle will become less and less, and you will grow more and more in Christ!

Show me your garden and I shall tell you
what you are.
—Alfred Austin

In With the New

We've learned that a seed must die in order for new life to spring forth. You might be thinking, "All this talk about death is a downer," and it would be, if that's where we kept our focus. But the brand-new life that breaks forth from the old seed shell is where we want to focus.

Let's carefully look at Colossians 3:1-4 and Galatians 2:20. Using your colored pencils, in both passages, cross out all the phrases related to death in red, and draw a yellow flower around all passages related to life.

> Since, then, you have been raised with Christ, set your hearts on things above, where Christ is seated at the right hand of God. Set your minds on things above, not on earthly things. For you died, and your life is now hidden with Christ in God. When Christ, who is your life, appears, then you also will appear with him in glory.
>
> —Colossians 3:1-4

I have been crucified with Christ and I no longer live, but Christ lives in me. The life I live in the body, I live by faith in the Son of God, who loved me and gave himself for me. —Galatians 2:20

Reflection:

1. What part of you is dead and has been "crucified with Christ"?

2. Whose life now lives in you?

3. How do we let the life of Christ live through us?

4. What should our minds be dwelling on?

As Christians, we have died to our sinful nature, and that's really good news! Christ's new life now replaces the old life. We are hidden in Him and our old seed coat is no longer recognizable—it's broken away so that the life of Christ can grow in and through us.

Begin today to set your mind on your *new life in Christ*. Remember the Rose Story. Jesus, the Rose of Sharon, wants you to think of yourself as a rose instead of a thistle. Our focus is always to look at Him. It's not about our old "selves" anymore. When we feel an "old pattern" creeping back into our lives, we need to fix our minds on Jesus and say to ourselves,

"I am His girl! I am a new creation in Christ! I no longer have to choose these old ways." We may have to do this many, many times, but each time we do, we are allowing the new growth to have its way in our lives, and we become strong in Christ.

Review the following two passages. Draw a flower around the word "new" and cross out anything related to the old:

> THEREFORE, IF ANYONE IS IN CHRIST, HE IS A NEW CREATION; THE OLD HAS GONE, THE NEW HAS COME! — 2 CORINTHIANS 5:17

> FORGET THE FORMER THINGS; DO NOT DWELL ON THE PAST. SEE, I AM DOING A NEW THING! NOW IT SPRINGS UP; DO YOU NOT PERCEIVE IT? I AM MAKING A WAY IN THE DESERT AND STREAMS IN THE WASTELAND.
> —ISAIAH 43:18-19

You are a new creation! You are not an old dead stump. You are a new green, flourishing plant full of life in Christ. The old you—that old sin nature—has been replaced with the powerful life of Christ, which is implanted, growing, and blooming in you. Forget the things of your past. God says they are dead and gone. When God looks at you He sees the new life of His Son—His Seed, Jesus Christ—growing within you, and He is *very pleased*. To Him, you look like His Son. Begin to see yourself the way God sees you. Focus on the "new you." There is a new shoot springing up in you every day! Now it springs up!

Look back at your answer to the third question regarding the Galatians passage. What is the "enzyme" that activates the new life to spring forth? It's faith! Our faith allows the new life to spring forth in our hearts. Think about the word "spring." Can you picture all of this energy and life just coiled up and ready to spring out and start living? What is this new life waiting on to set it free to spring forth with incredible joy? It's waiting on you to *believe*. Believe what God says about you. Believe His Word!

Here's an exercise that will help you really know what God says about you in His Word. Refer to the Seed Packets of Truth in the back of this book. Find the cards "Seeds for Your New Life" and choose five Scriptures from those cards that are really important to you. Write them down in the space that follows. Plant these seeds of truth into your garden and water them daily with faith.

Vi's Gardening Tip:

Tear out the "Seeds for Your New Life" cards found at the end of the book. Keep them with you in your book bag or purse. Let them be your spiritual mirrors. When you look at these verses, you are looking at your image—your reflection. This is who you are! Don't forget it. Take them with you and look at them often. Memorize some or all of the verses. Learn to know what you look like—how God sees you. When you are tempted to dwell on your old "self," get out your mirror (God's Word) and look long and hard!

For as the soil makes the sprout come up and a garden causes seeds to grow, so the Sovereign LORD will make righteousness and praise spring up before all nations.

—Isaiah 61:11

Lesson Fifteen

Rooted in Christ

Roots are essential to the life of any plant. During the germination process of a seed, the tip of the root is the *first* part of the new plant that surfaces. Why? Because the root *anchors* the seed in place, enabling the seed to thrive and grow. Take a tree, for instance. The roots are the foundation of the tree—supporting, grounding, and securing it. The roots must keep growing underground and unseen as the tree grows in stature aboveground. If a tree is not firmly rooted, it will topple when storms beat against it. Roots also draw water and nutrients from the soil, which are essential ingredients for the growth of a plant.

Without strong, healthy roots, a plant has little chance for survival. This truth also applies to our spiritual lives. Believers need strong, healthy *spiritual* roots in order to grow and stand strong and secure during the storms of life.

Look up the following Scriptures and fill in the missing words. Pay special attention to the mention of our spiritual roots. (Note: The following Scriptures are from the New International Version of the Bible. Other translations may differ.)

Ephesians 3:17-19:

"And I pray that you, being ______________ and ______________

in ______________, may have ______________, together with all

THE SAINTS, TO GRASP HOW ______________ AND ______________ AND ______________ AND ______________ IS THE ______________ OF ______________, AND TO KNOW THIS ______________ THAT SURPASSES KNOWLEDGE—THAT YOU MAY BE ______________ TO THE MEASURE OF ALL THE ______________ OF GOD."

COLOSSIANS 2:6-7:

"SO THEN, JUST AS YOU ______________ CHRIST JESUS AS LORD, __________ TO LIVE IN HIM, ______________________ AND ____________________ IN HIM, ____________________ IN THE FAITH AS YOU WERE TAUGHT, AND, ______________________ WITH, ________________________."

How do we grow these spiritual roots that the Bible speaks of? Let's take a look.

First, Christ, the Seed, is implanted in our hearts through faith when we invite Him to come and dwell within us, making Him Lord of our lives. Then, we are to become *rooted and grounded in His love* as Ephesians 3:17-19 says. But how, you might ask?

The answer may sound easy, but it takes faith, and in most cases, requires daily contending (actively fighting) to hold our ground. You see, in order to become rooted and grounded in God's love we must *choose to believe* God's Word. God's great love for us is mentioned over and over again throughout the Bible. This choosing to believe in His love is an act of our *will*. It's more than an emotion or a feeling. It is a conviction of truth: You *know* God's love for you to be true, even though at times you don't *feel* it. When we know and believe that we are completely and totally loved by God, we are rooted and grounded (firmly established), and able to be filled with the fullness of God (Ephesians 3:19).

Reflection:

Our feelings are fickle, but God's truths are immovable. Do you have days when you *feel* that God doesn't love you? What can you do (or say to yourself) on those days to encourage yourself that God truly does love you? Write your thoughts below:

The love of God brings nourishment to our souls and flows through us to others. Our roots must go deep to know the breadth, length, height, and depth of His love. Notice that the description of love in the above Ephesians passage uses four dimensions: wide, long, high, and deep. We live in a 3-dimensional world: long, wide, high. This extra dimension to God's love places it in a realm beyond our limited human understanding. It speaks of the eternal dimension. That's what verse 19 refers to by saying this love *surpasses knowledge*. It doesn't mean we can't know God's love; it just means we will never fully understand it, because it is so great and immeasurable. Let's look more closely at each dimension to gain a better understanding of this infinite, eternal love of God.

Width: God loves all people, all races, all denominations, and both male or female, regardless of position or status. He loves the righteous and the wicked. His love has no discrimination, no boundaries, and no barriers. His love encompasses us all. He desires all to be saved. Look up 1 Timothy 2:4 and write it below:

Length: God's love has no end. It is unfailing, steadfast, and ever-present. You see, nothing can separate you from God's love. Look up Psalm 100:5 and write it below. Note: Your Bible translation may use the word "mercy" instead of "love":

Height: God's love is immeasurable, is unlimited, and reaches as high as the heavens. Can you measure the heavens? Neither can you measure God's love. Look up Psalm 57:10 and write it here:

Depth: God's love is unconditional. He loves you just as you are. There is nothing you can do to earn His love. You already have it. *There is nothing you can do to make Him stop loving you.* He has always loved you, and He always will. You have a choice to turn from Him and reject His love, but His love will always be constant and true. Look up Romans 5:8 and write it below:

Now look at the illustration of the tree's root system. Fill in the corresponding Scriptures (width, length, height, and depth) from above into the designated "roots" and write down the main truth about God's love. Use this picture to remind yourself of the importance of being rooted and secured in God's love.

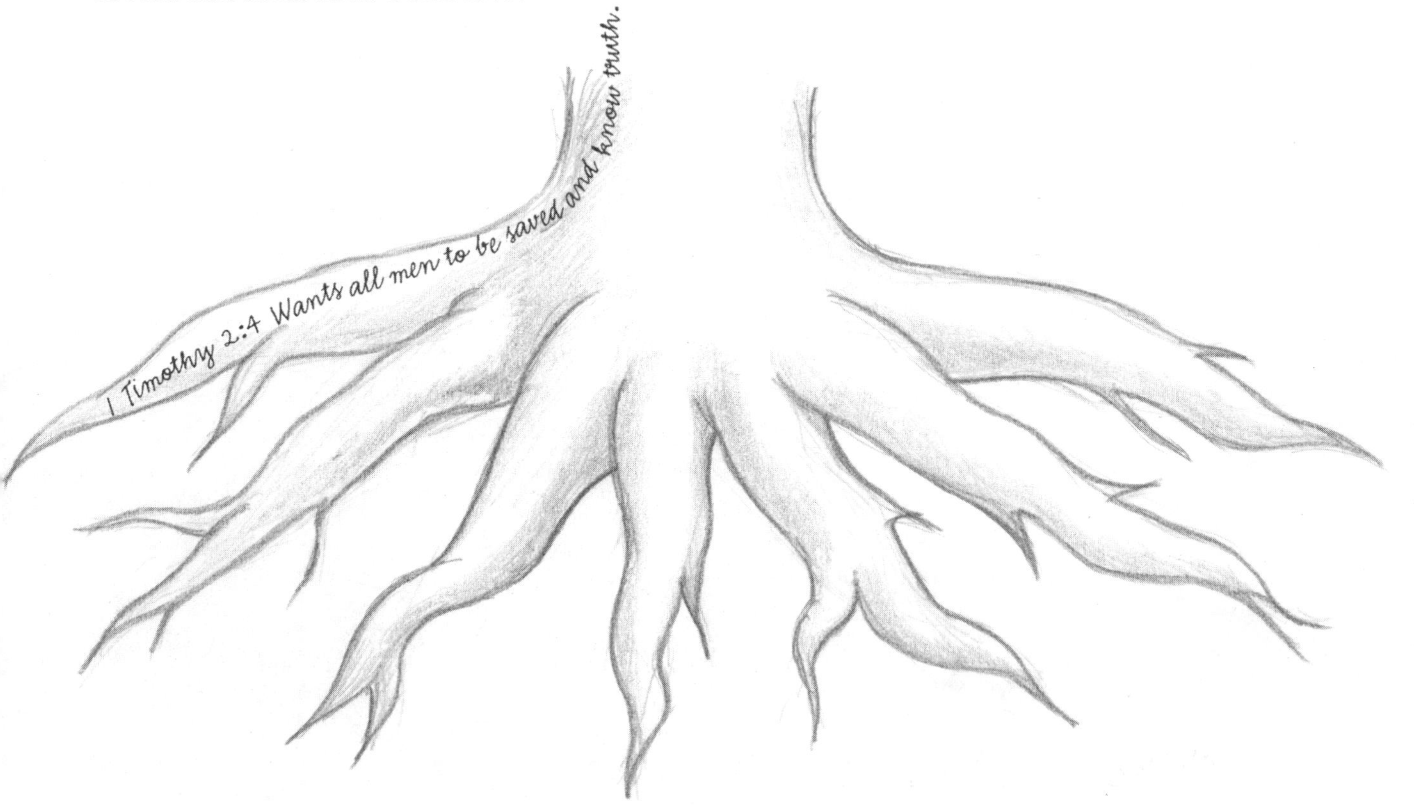

1 Timothy 2:4 Wants all men to be saved and know truth.

Notice how the most important part of the tree is hidden beneath the ground. So it is in our lives. Our faith is like the root system of a large tree: You can't see it, but it must be large enough and deep enough to be that solid foundation for your life.

Roots secure a plant. If we are rooted in Christ, we will be secure within ourselves. Love is the deepest, most vital need that human beings have. We are all created with a need for love and a sense of belonging. Unfortunately, all humans are flawed and can never provide for one another the level of love and acceptance that our hearts crave. God, on the other hand, is perfect, and He loves us with a perfect love. When we truly understand the depth of God's love for us, we can stop trying to fill that void with the things of this world. We will no longer fear loneliness and rejection. We won't fear the opinions of men. His perfect love will make us secure and no longer afraid.

Vi's Gardening Tip:

For strong, thriving spiritual roots, settle in your heart first, foremost, and forevermore that your Heavenly Father *loves you*. You are loved by God. Nothing can separate you from His love. Allow this transforming truth to be the "tip of the root" that surfaces first from the spiritual seed in your heart. Embracing the Father's love for you will anchor you in Christ, and He in you. As the above verses exhort, be rooted and established in *love*; be rooted and built up in Christ. Let not your heart ever doubt the Master Gardener's unwavering love for you!

Kind hearts are the garden,
kind thoughts are the root,
kind words are the blossoms,
kind deeds are the fruit.
—Author Unknown

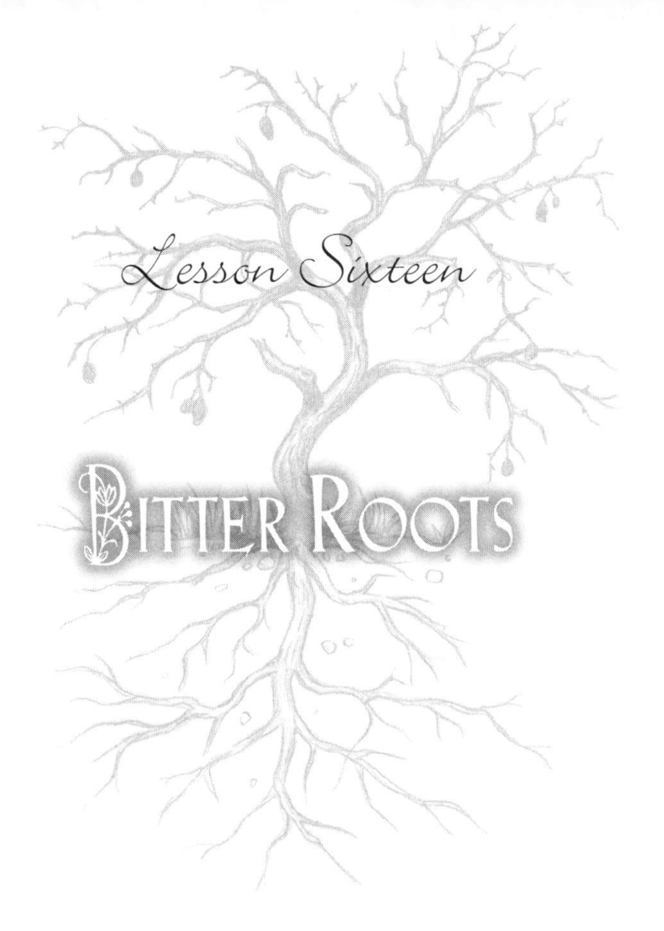

If your spiritual roots aren't tapping into the reservoir of Christ's love to receive their nutrients, they may become bitter and poison your spiritual growth. Bitter roots produce bitter fruit, which is harmful to self and others. Let's learn a bit more about what the Bible has to say about bitter roots. Hebrews 12:15 says:

> SEE TO IT THAT NO ONE MISSES THE GRACE OF GOD AND THAT NO BITTER ROOT GROWS UP TO CAUSE TROUBLE AND DEFILE MANY. —HEBREWS 12:15

What does *defile* mean? Use a dictionary and/or thesaurus to look up the meaning of this word. Write the definition below:

As you can see, bitter roots will cause unclean and foul growth in our lives, which in turn can even cause trouble and poison others. Do you want the garden of your soul, where Jesus walks and communes with you, to be contaminated with putrid fruit? Read Ephesians 4:31-32. Underline the bitter "fruits" listed in this Scripture.

> GET RID OF ALL BITTERNESS, RAGE AND ANGER, BRAWLING AND SLANDER, ALONG WITH EVERY FORM OF MALICE. BE KIND AND COMPASSIONATE TO ONE ANOTHER, FORGIVING EACH OTHER, JUST AS IN CHRIST GOD FORGAVE YOU. —EPHESIANS 4:31-32

In the diagram below, write in the bitter fruits you underlined in the passage above. What are some other bitter fruits you can think of? Add them to the diagram also.

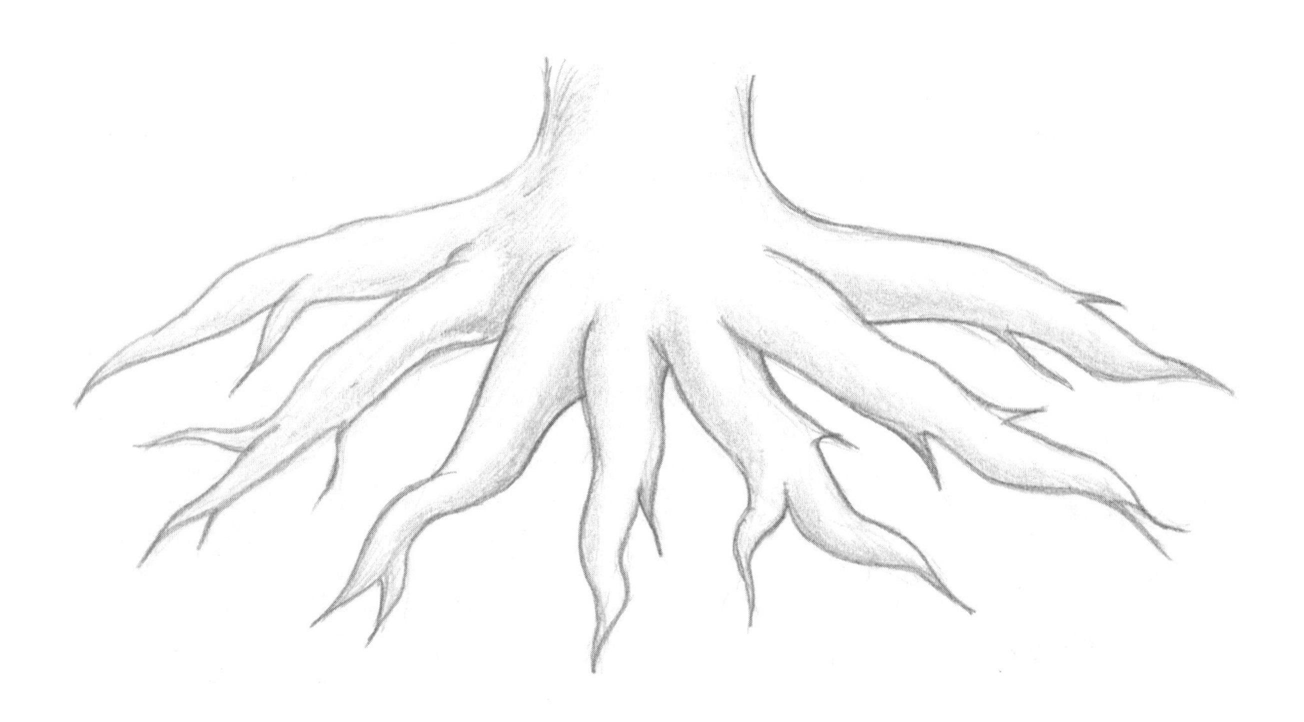

How can these bitter fruits be harmful to you and to those around you? (For example, when I gossip about another girl, it destroys my reputation and is hurtful and embarrassing to the girl.)

Whenever these and other such fruit are being produced in your life, you probably have a root of bitterness. Roots of bitterness can spring up at any time, so we have to watch out for them. The most common source or cause for the root of bitterness is unforgiveness and resentment. These are like a poisonous reservoir in which bitter roots grow. If you are not securely rooted and secured in the reservoir of Christ's love—spreading out and drinking in the fullness of the width, length, depth, and height of His great love—then you can easily become offended and resentful toward others when they sin against you. The primary way to truly uproot these bitter roots is to concentrate on really knowing the love of Christ, like we studied in our previous lesson. When you really understand how Christ loves you, you can then love others the same way.

Let's look at 1 Peter 3:8 and at Colossians 3:12-13:

> FINALLY, ALL OF YOU, LIVE IN HARMONY WITH ONE ANOTHER; BE SYMPATHETIC, LOVE AS BROTHERS, BE COMPASSIONATE AND HUMBLE.
>
> —1 PETER 3:8

> THEREFORE, AS THE ELECT OF GOD, HOLY AND BELOVED, PUT ON TENDER MERCIES, KINDNESS, HUMILITY, MEEKNESS, LONGSUFFERING; BEARING WITH ONE ANOTHER, AND FORGIVING ONE ANOTHER, IF ANYONE HAS A COMPLAINT AGAINST ANOTHER; EVEN AS CHRIST FORGAVE YOU, SO YOU ALSO MUST DO. —COLOSSIANS 3:12-13 (NEW KING JAMES VERSION)

Draw a star around the qualities you see in these verses that will help you to forgive. (These good qualities are like "minerals" that enrich the soil of your heart!)

What do these two Scriptures tell you about forgiveness?

Do you fully believe that Christ has forgiven you and continues to forgive you when you confess your sin? Can you believe that He will also help you forgive others? Write your thoughts below:

Forgiving is probably one of the hardest things God asks us to do. Oftentimes we cannot forgive a person in our own strength. But if you will make the *decision to forgive*, God's love and power will be readily available to help you do so. Stretch your spiritual roots down and drink deeply of Christ's love. Every time you begin to think of the wrong done to you, think about how Christ has forgiven you for your sins. Remember how Christ Himself was mistreated, and how on the Cross He asked the Father to forgive His enemies. With compassion, Jesus understood that they didn't know what they were doing. Luke 6:36 says, "Be merciful, just as your Father is merciful."

You can see those who have offended you through the same compassion and mercy of Christ. You can begin to understand that they have acted hurtfully because they themselves are hurting, whether they realize it or not. They are struggling with their own bitter roots. Begin to pray a blessing over their lives, and you will eventually find your own anger and pain begin to dissolve.

Are there roots of unforgiveness and resentment in the soil of your heart? Make a list of the people toward whom you feel unforgiveness or resentment, and how those negative feelings have affected you. (It may even be yourself whom you are struggling to forgive.)

Person's Name	Wrong Committed Against Me	My Resulting Heart Condition
Sarah	*Lied about me to a friend*	*I felt hurt and angry*

Here is a simple prayer you can pray for each person on your list:

DEAR HEAVENLY FATHER,

MY HEART IS REALLY HURTING RIGHT NOW BECAUSE ________________ HAS WRONGED ME. THANK YOU FOR REVEALING THESE ROOTS OF UNFORGIVENESS IN MY HEART, FOR I DO NOT WANT ANYTHING TO HINDER MY RELATIONSHIP WITH YOU. AS HARD AS IT IS FOR ME RIGHT NOW, I'M ASKING IF YOU COULD PLEASE TAKE MY EMOTIONS—ANGER, DISAPPOINTMENT,

SORROW, AND UNFORGIVENESS—AND GIVE ME YOUR HEART OF MERCY, FORGIVENESS, AND LOVE FOR THIS PERSON. I KNOW THAT I CANNOT DO THIS IN MY OWN STRENGTH, SO I AM ASKING FOR A MIRACLE OF FORGIVENESS FROM YOU. TEACH ME MORE ABOUT YOUR LOVE AND YOUR WAYS IN THESE HURTFUL SITUATIONS, AND HELP ME TO BE SENSITIVE TOWARD OTHERS. THANK YOU FOR FORGIVING MY SINS AND FOR HELPING ME TO FORGIVE OTHERS. NOW, LORD, I PRAY THAT YOU WOULD BLESS __________ AND HELP HIM/HER REALLY UNDERSTAND HOW MUCH YOU LOVE HIM/HER. AND LET YOUR LOVE WASH AWAY THE HURTFUL PLACES IN BOTH OF OUR HEARTS. IN JESUS' PRECIOUS NAME I PRAY—AMEN.

Note: Sometimes you may have bitterness and anger toward God. Be honest with Him and confess how you feel. He is big enough to handle it. If you are angry at God for something that has happened to you (or that didn't happen), begin to trust that He will cause something beautiful to grow in the wilderness places of your life. We will discuss this more in Lesson 24—Your Wilderness Will Bloom!

Vi's Gardening Tip:

Ask your Master Gardener to search the garden of your heart for any roots of bitterness and then work together with Him in pulling every one of them out. Pray this prayer from Psalm 139:23-24: "Search me, O God, and know my heart; test me and know my anxious thoughts. See if there is any offensive way in me, and lead me in the way everlasting."

Keep your garden pure and undefiled. It takes hard work to go after these bitter roots, but having a fragrant, refreshing garden is well worth the effort! We will talk more about fruit later, but remember: Fruit is meant to be eaten. What you produce in the garden of your soul is not only consumed by you, but also by others with whom you come in contact with.

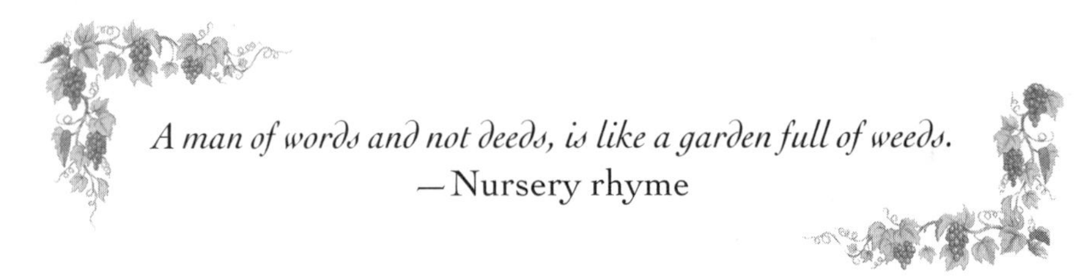

A man of words and not deeds, is like a garden full of weeds.
—Nursery rhyme

Lesson Seventeen

ABIDING

In Lesson 12—Working in Your Garden, we finished the lesson by reading Isaiah 55:9-11, which said that God's Word does not return to Him without accomplishing the purposes for which He sends it. Isn't it reassuring to know that God is committed to our growth and that the seeds of truth and promises found in His Word *will* grow inside of us, eventually producing a bountiful crop in our lives? We do not need to be burdened and troubled by disbelief and discouragement. Instead, we can learn to fully and joyfully *rest* in fellowship (friendship) with Christ as we wait for signs of our new growth. And that is what we will look at today—the vital importance of "abiding" in Christ.

Joy

Abiding is the most important principle regarding fruit bearing, which we will study in our next lesson. To *abide* means to rest or dwell, to remain, to continue to be sure or firm, to endure. Simply put, abiding in Christ means resting in your intimate, personal relationship with the Lord.

In light of this definition, let's look at John 15:4-8. Please circle the word "remain" each time you see it. Make a box around the phrase "bear fruit" or "bear much fruit."

REMAIN IN ME, AND I WILL REMAIN IN YOU. NO BRANCH CAN BEAR FRUIT BY ITSELF; IT MUST REMAIN IN THE VINE. NEITHER CAN YOU BEAR FRUIT UNLESS YOU REMAIN IN ME. I AM THE VINE; YOU ARE THE BRANCHES. IF A MAN REMAINS IN ME AND I IN HIM, HE WILL BEAR MUCH FRUIT; APART FROM ME YOU CAN DO NOTHING. IF ANYONE DOES NOT REMAIN IN ME, HE IS LIKE A BRANCH THAT IS THROWN AWAY AND WITHERS; SUCH BRANCHES ARE PICKED UP, THROWN INTO THE FIRE AND BURNED. IF YOU REMAIN IN ME AND MY WORDS REMAIN IN YOU, ASK WHATEVER YOU WISH, AND IT WILL BE GIVEN YOU. THIS IS TO MY FATHER'S GLORY, THAT YOU BEAR MUCH FRUIT, SHOWING YOURSELVES TO BE MY DISCIPLES. —JOHN 15:4-8

Based on your observations of this passage, how important is it to Christ that His disciples remain, or abide, in Him?

What did Jesus say would happen as a result of abiding in Him?

Notice the connection you made between abiding (remaining) and fruit bearing. Abiding in Christ *will* lead to fruitfulness. They go hand in hand. Here's a "gardening formula" to remember: ABIDING IN CHRIST=FRUIT BEARING

Look at the first sentence in John 15:4 and fill in the blanks:

Who remains (abides) in Christ? ___________________________

Who remains (abides) in you? ___________________________

To abide in Christ is to rest in the knowledge and understanding that Christ's life *also* abides in *you*. This is the oneness we have with Christ—as you abide in Christ, He abides in you. We are beautifully intertwined and connected to the life of Christ.

Jesus used this analogy of a vine and branches as a way to help us understand a very important principle in our relationship with Him: On its own, a branch cannot produce life and fruit. The sap, which provides the life of the plant, flows from the roots to the vine and then into the branches. What do you suppose would happen to a branch if it were cut off from the grapevine and lost its supply of the sap? Would the severed branch continue to grow juicy, red grapes? Hardly! In just a few hours, it would begin to shrivel up and die, leaving no life left in the branch. The branch can only live if it is attached to the vine where it can receive its nourishment and life. Well, we are like those branches and the sap is the life of Christ—His Holy Spirit—flowing from Christ and into our lives. We can only grow delicious, luscious fruit if we are abiding in Christ, letting His Spirit flow to and through us.

To be truly fruitful in our lives, we must learn to "be" with Christ. We must learn to let Him "be" through us. Learn "to be" before you worry about the "to do." Rest assured that you will grow, mature, and become fruitful in your Christian life as you learn to abide (or rest) in Christ. The greater the rest, the greater the fruit.

Based on what you've learned so far in this lesson, do you have any guesses as to *how* we abide in Christ in our daily lives? Write your thoughts below:

There are many ways we can keep our relationship with Christ growing and thriving (refer to Lesson 12—Working in Your Garden), such as through our personal devotional times, fellowship with others, prayer, worship, and living out God's guidelines. But abiding is different. When we abide in Christ, we don't have to "do" anything except to simply rest, enjoy, and believe everything God has done for us through Christ. Think about it: Christ has accomplished everything we need for our salvation and everything we need to experience the fullness of His life—and that means now, not when we die and go to Heaven! We can enjoy the fullness of His life this very moment. We have not done nor can we do one thing to accomplish this. Christ did it all. Christ must still do it all. We must learn to depend on Him for everything, just as the branch is dependent on the vine.

To illustrate, imagine that you have been tossed into stormy ocean waters wearing a life jacket. To abide is to trust that the life jacket will keep you afloat. You must put your faith in the life jacket and "rest" against it, surrendering yourself to it and allowing it to sustain and carry you. Not to abide is to thrash your arms and legs around in the water, resisting the buoyancy of the jacket. You expend your energy needlessly and become fearful and anxious. Whether you abide or not, the "life jacket" will always keep you afloat. So why not relax and reap the benefits of abiding in Christ, rather than striving against it?

Reflection:

Abiding is something we must learn to do because it oftentimes does not come naturally in our busy lives. As humans, we are prone to go through our days in a flurry of our own strength with our own goals and agendas. Abiding requires that we take time to drink in the sap of the life of Christ—the Holy Spirit. We can quickly turn our thoughts to God and take sips throughout our day, but it is crucial that we carve out some time to really take a good long drink from our water supply! When we do, we will be amazed at how refreshed and energized we become.

One of the best ways to take a good long drink is to learn to meditate. To meditate means to reflect deeply on or to think intently about something. Meditation is often mentioned in the Bible. David makes several references to thinking deeply and reflecting on God, His Word, and His works:

> But his delight is in the law of the Lord, and on his law he meditates day and night. —Psalm 1:2

> On my bed I remember you; I think of you through the watches of the night. —Psalm 63:6

> My eyes stay open through the watches of the night, that I may meditate on your promises. —Psalm 119:148

> They will speak of the glorious splendor of your majesty, and I will meditate on your wonderful works. —Psalm 145:5

Take several minutes to go through the exercise called "Quieting Yourself in God's Presence" at the end of this lesson. Retreat to the garden of your heart and quiet yourself before God.

Vi's Gardening Tip:

Take time today to go outside and observe a tree, plant, vine, or shrub. What strikes you the most about the relationship between the branches and the trunk, or the branches and the vines? Does it appear that the branches are striving and fretting to stay connected to the tree limbs or vines? Really, the branches just "are." It is a truly wonderful relationship that the vine and the branches share. Record your observations in a journal and ask your Master Gardener to teach you the simple yet profound principle of abiding in Christ.

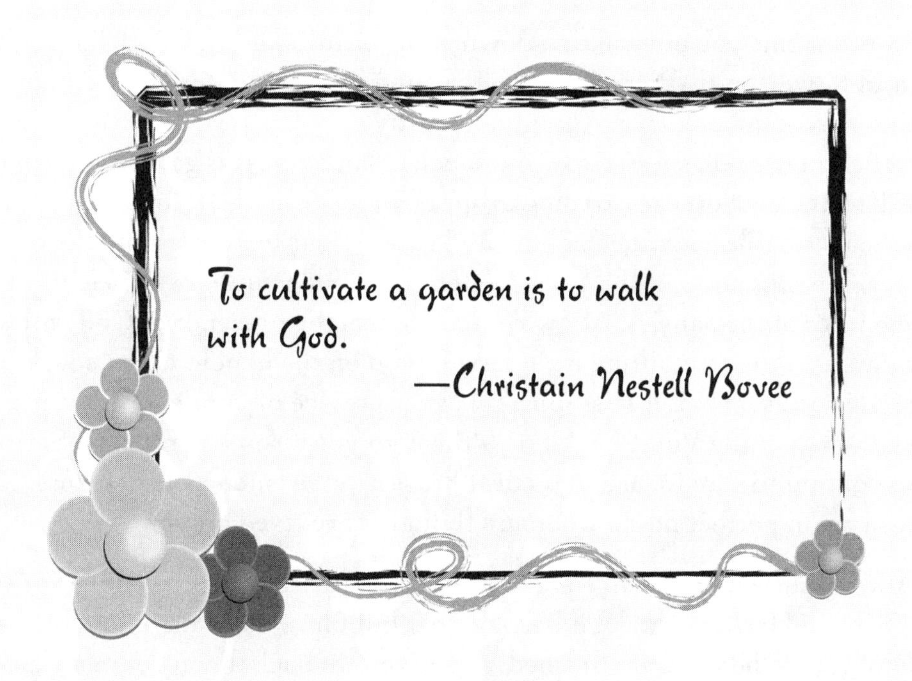

To cultivate a garden is to walk with God.
—Christain Nestell Bovee

Quieting Yourself in God's Presence

~ Meditation in the Garden ~

As we've mentioned, gardens offer a wonderful retreat for relaxing and meditating on the presence of God. You can find a real garden to sit in and meditate or you can use your wonderful imagination to picture a garden in your mind. The goal is quieting yourself in God's presence and enjoying His love.

Before you start, pick a very quiet place where you will relax. Quiet your mind. Set aside your worldly concerns and focus on God (attach yourself to your Vine).

Now imagine you are walking down your beautiful garden path lined with shade trees and flower beds. Picture yourself sitting on a bench in your garden under a beautiful spreading oak tree. A fountain lightly splashes nearby. Use all five of your senses (hearing, smell, sight, taste, and touch) to imagine this garden experience with Jesus. Feel the cool breeze carrying drops of water from the fountain onto your face. Smell the incredible fragrance of lilies and roses. Hear the birds sing, the breeze in the trees, the humming of the bees. Watch the golden sunlight dance off of the bobbing faces of the pansies. Allow yourself to feel the presence of God with you or imagine that Jesus is sitting right next to you on the bench. Don't speak, just drink in His presence. Let His Spirit fill every crevice of your soul. This is a time to receive the sap of the Vine! Feel it flow through you! You can repeat a Scripture to help your mind stay focused, or paraphrase a verse, such as Isaiah 26:3: "You will keep me in perfect peace when my thoughts are fixed on you."

Allow yourself plenty of time to linger there with Jesus, the lover of your soul. Drink in His love and let it become that bubbling fountain of joy flowing out of you. When you are finished, as you retreat back down your garden path, try to keep the peace you have experienced from being swallowed up by worldly cares.

Again, this is a discipline which will require practice. It will get easier the more you do it. We must actually train our minds to turn away from the cares of life and center in on our Master Gardener. It's well worth it, because this is how we stay fresh, flourishing, and fruitful.

In the Garden

I come to the garden alone
While the dew is still on the roses
And the voice I hear falling on my ear
The Son of God discloses.

Refrain

And He walks with me, and He talks with me,
And He tells me I am His own;
And the joy we share as we tarry there,
None other has ever known.

He speaks, and the sound of His voice,
Is so sweet the birds hush their singing,
And the melody that He gave to me
Within my heart is ringing.

Refrain

I'd stay in the garden with Him
Though the night around me be falling,
But He bids me go; through the voice of woe
His voice to me is calling.

By Charles Austin Miles (1868-1946)

Your Master Gardener is looking and longing for fruitfulness from your garden. It is a sign that the life of Christ is growing healthy and strong in you—that the Seed of Christ is producing the fruit of Christ in your life. The Master Gardener will have a wonderful harvest from your life—a harvest which He will multiply to be used to help others and to spread the good news of the gospel.

What exactly is fruitfulness in the life of a believer? It is the *good works* that glorify God. What do you think these good works are? Write your thoughts below:

Good works are any acts of service, kindness, or help we may do for others, or any words of encouragement we speak to lift others up. Some examples of good works could be raking a neighbor's yard, encouraging a hurting friend, or opening the door for an elderly person. Anytime you are able to demonstrate the love of God to another and point him or her to God, you are doing a "good work."

Read the following verses very carefully. Using your colored pencils, underline the phrase "good work." Next, circle the word "fruit."

Colossians 1:10

And we pray this in order that you may live a life worthy of the Lord and may please Him in every way: bearing fruit in every good work, growing in the knowledge of God.

John 15:8

This is to my Father's glory, that you bear much fruit, showing yourselves to be my disciples.

Ephesians 2:10

For we are God's workmanship, created in Christ Jesus to do good works, which God prepared in advance for us to do.

John 15:16

You did not choose me, but I chose you and appointed you to go and bear fruit—fruit that will last. Then the Father will give you whatever you ask in my name.

Through these verses it's clear to see that God has planned for us to bear fruit by doing good works through His Son, Jesus. The good works we perform are done "in Christ" or "through Christ"—that is, through the Holy Spirit who lives in us. Someone has said, "God's Spirit is in us and He wants out!" The "good works" are the natural results of Christ's Spirit being released *through* us.

If we are to experience freedom and joy in Christ, we must understand that we cannot earn God's favor or love or our salvation by doing good works. We don't have to go running around in a frenzy trying to please God the Father by doing a bunch of good deeds. If we have Jesus, we are already righteous and pleasing in God's sight. We are saved by believing in the work of salvation that Christ has done for us through His death and resurrection. *Fruit bearing is not about earning our salvation or God's blessings; it's about letting the Seed of God grow and bloom in us!* Remember our study on seeds? Seeds *will* produce some kind of fruit. The Seed of God, growing healthy and strong in you, will naturally produce fruit in your life. And that fruit will come in the form of good works.

This beautiful work of fruit bearing is a partnership between you and your Master Gardener. Philippians 2:12-13 and Hebrews 13:20-21 show this beautiful balance between God's work and ours. Read the following verses. Underline the word "work" in green if it's God's work, and write "God" above it. Underline the word "work" or "works" in blue if it is your work, and write "mine" above it. Draw a purple flower around the word "good" each time it appears.

Philippians 2:12-13

Therefore, my dear friends, as you have always obeyed—not only in my presence, but now much more in my absence—continue to work out your salvation with fear and trembling, for it is God who works in you to will and to act according to his good purpose.

Hebrews 13:20-21

May the God of peace, who through the blood of the eternal covenant brought back from the dead our Lord Jesus, that great Shepherd of the sheep, equip you with everything good for doing his will, and may he work in us what is pleasing to him, through Jesus Christ, to whom be glory for ever and ever. Amen.

What is God's work that is mentioned in the verses above?

Look back at Ephesians 2:10. God has planned good works for you to do. It is His responsibility (His work) to give you what you need to do those good works.

What is it that God has given you which will accomplish every good work in your life?

Yes, you know the answer—His Son and His Holy Spirit. Through His Spirit, He is forming and growing the life of Christ within you, and the fruit of Jesus' life is the "good works." So then, what is our work mentioned in Philippians 2:12?

Our work is to let the life of Christ flow out from us. How? Through faith, nurturing our relationship with Christ, and our willingness to be used by the Master Gardener. Our work is an extension of His work in us—a natural flowing out of what is within. Our work is to cling to Christ, our Vine, and to release the life of Christ everywhere we go. Therefore, our focus for fruit bearing must always be on nurturing the life of Christ within us (abiding in Him) and then responding to opportunities to do good when they come our way.

Be prepared and watch for these opportunities for good works. They will come in the daily events of your life. Don't just be looking for the big and grandiose works. God may bring those along, but usually your God-appointed good works unfold in simple and natural ways as you live each and every day. For instance, look for ways you can help your mom (like emptying the dishwasher or clearing the dinner table). If a friend is having a bad day, take a minute to give her a smile and pray for her. Offer to let your brother or sister choose which movie to watch or which game to play over your own personal interests.

Think back on yesterday. Was there an opportunity for some good work (whether small or large) that you either missed or seized? Write your experience below:

In doing good works we must never separate ourselves from Jesus. Remember our abiding verse in John 15, "Apart from Him, we can do nothing." You can rest in the law of the seed. The seed grows and produces its life and fruit. The Seed of God grows and produces His life and fruit in you. The fruit is good works. And God will harvest this fruit, whether small or large, and use it for His glory.

Vi's Gardening Tip:

An apple tree doesn't grunt, groan, or sweat to make apples. It merely puts down deep roots and receives water and nutrients from the soil. The fruit comes naturally. So don't strive to bear fruit—seek to know your Gardener. Worship Him. Love and enjoy Him. Let Him become your complete joy, and you will be a fruitful tree for Him.

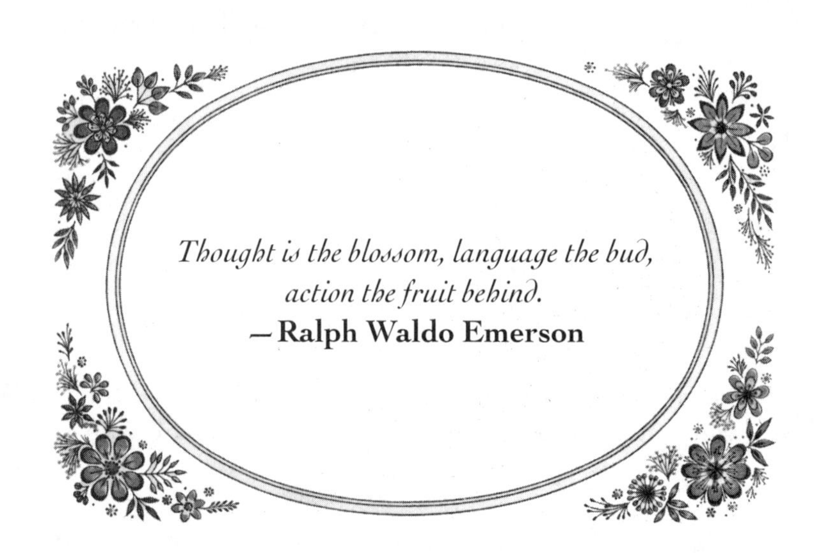

Thought is the blossom, language the bud,
action the fruit behind.
—Ralph Waldo Emerson

Lesson Nineteen

Pruning

As we learn the peaceful and strengthening practice of abiding in Christ, we can be assured that over time we will begin to notice fruit, growth, and change produced in our lives. Just as any plant or vine gradually grows stronger and healthier as it stays connected to its source, so will we grow stronger and healthier as we stay connected to our source, Jesus Christ, the true vine. But with growth, there must also be maintenance.

Have you ever seen an unsupervised rose bush? If not tended to regularly, a rose bush will grow wild and unruly, with prickly shoots that will eventually use up most, if not all, of the nutrients from the main stalk, leaving the other branches undernourished and unhealthy. Even a basic backyard lawn must be mowed and trimmed regularly, otherwise the grass becomes too long and weeds pop up, creating a real mess.

The same is true for our spiritual growth. As we grow and mature in spiritual matters, there will be times when some of our own "branches" must be cut back and trimmed. This process is called *pruning*. Every gardener knows that to neglect to prune is to neglect the garden. Pruning is necessary for a plant to grow healthy, strong, and full of fruit.

While Jesus is the vine and we are the branches, let's remind ourselves who tends this eternal garden. Look up John 15:1-2 and write it below:

What does the Gardener do to make the branch more fruitful? Write your answer below:

Pruning is the cutting away of straggly, immature, or even dead branches in order to improve the shape and/or growth of a plant. In delightful contrast, pruning also involves cutting back healthy branches so that they will become even stronger and more fruitful! *Pruning is for both the sickly and healthy branches.* Pruning is done out of great love and care for the plant's well-being. Out of His perfect love and His desire to see the fullness of Christ's life come forth in us, God will prune the garden of your soul. He will faithfully and lovingly sever from you that which hinders and entangles the growth of the life of Christ in your life. He will also cut back those areas of strength in order for you to become stronger.

Stop for a moment and think about areas in your life that are weaknesses, or things that may be hindering your spiritual growth. Are there any dead, immature, or weak branches that the Master Gardener may need to prune back? (Some examples could be if you have a tendency to become easily offended, to gossip, to fear, or to harbor negative thoughts.) If you're not sure, ask Him to reveal those areas to you now. Write your insights below:

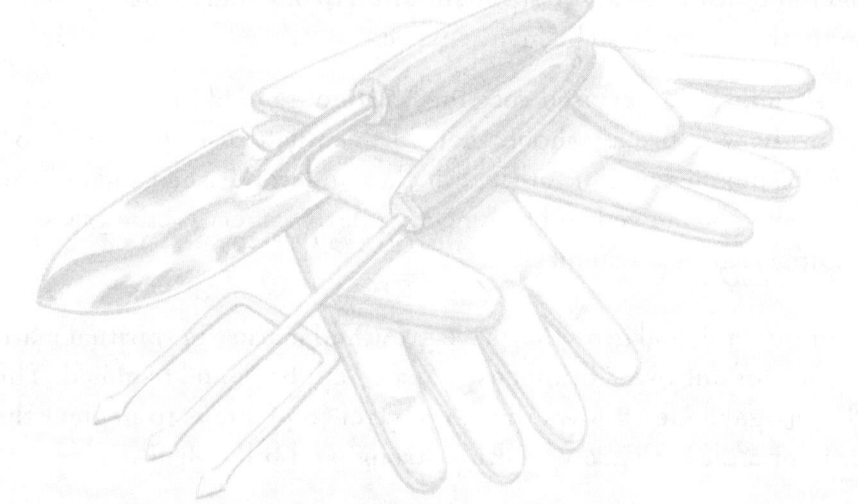

Why would God sometimes prune back our strengths? Let's consider this: Suppose someone has a strong gift of leadership, but struggles with being bossy and controlling. The pruning process can help develop the leadership gift by making him or her more patient with others and less selfish or willful.

Now think about your areas of strength. List a few of your strengths below. Consider how God might prune back your strengths in order to ensure greater growth in those areas:

During seasons of pruning it is easy for us to misunderstand the process. When we feel the pain of the Gardener's shears, we may begin to think that God is mad at us or that we are being punished for some sin. This is simply not true. *Your Gardener sees great potential in you for a wonderful harvest. It is because He is pleased with you that He prunes your garden.*

How does God prune us? He may use circumstances in our lives to touch an area that reveals our weaknesses, as well as discipline, tests and trials, or suffering and sorrows of various kinds. Either way, we should not despair when God begins to move in our lives in this way.

Here is an example of how the pruning process might work: Suppose you have a tendency to be critical or judgmental toward others. You are quick to point out other people's weaknesses or flaws. God might prune this from your life by allowing a circumstance in which someone else begins to criticize you and point out your flaws. From this experience, you will know how awful and hurtful it feels to be on the receiving end of criticism. Your heart becomes tender and merciful toward others, and you are less likely to be quick to criticize. Thus the painful pruning process has done its good work in your life!

REFLECTION:

Times of pruning can be difficult. But the results far outweigh the tests. When we endure the pruning process, it will produce a harvest of righteousness and peace in our lives. Let's examine Hebrews 12:5-11:

"MY SON, THINK OF THE LORD'S TRAINING AS IMPORTANT. DO NOT LOSE HOPE WHEN HE CORRECTS YOU. THE LORD TRAINS THOSE HE LOVES. HE PUNISHES EVERYONE HE ACCEPTS AS A SON." PUT UP WITH HARD TIMES.

God uses them to train you. He is treating you as children. What children are not trained by their parents? God trains all of his children. But what if he doesn't train you? Then you are like children of people who weren't married to each other. You are not truly God's children.

Besides, we have all had human parents who trained us. We respected them for it. How much more should we be trained by the Father of our spirits and live! Our parents trained us for a little while. They did what they thought was best. But God trains us for our good. He wants us to share in his holiness. No training seems pleasant at the time. In fact, it seems painful. But later on it produces a harvest of godliness and peace. It does that for those who have been trained by it. —Hebrews 12:5-11 (New International Reader's Version)

What do you think God is accomplishing in your life through pruning?

How does pruning (correction, training) show that God truly loves you and wants the best for you?

What is the fruit of God's pruning in our life?

What quality must you have in order to benefit from this training? (We studied this in our soil chapter on hardened paths.)

The Hebrews 12 passage says that true caring and loving parents will train and correct (discipline) their children because it is for their good. God is a perfect, loving Father and you are His child through the Seed of Christ growing within you. He cares very much that you grow to be a healthy, strong, and fruitful tree of righteousness. He knows that as you grow, you need to be corrected, trained, and instructed, as any son or daughter does. He cares enough for our good that He will take great pains to discipline and teach.

In the natural world, a vine will grow in whatever direction it wants if it is not watched over. If the gardener wants the vine to climb a fence or trellis, he must train it by cutting off branches and repeatedly forcing the stubborn vine to go the way he wants it to. This is how your Master Gardener uses pruning in your life. In love, He will cut away and trim back areas that are stubborn or in the way of His good purpose for you.

This is how He teaches and trains us. We can be hopeful in our times of pruning because we know that God always trains us for our good. We can trust that the outcome will be an incredible increase of His holiness, and a sure harvest of godliness and peace. But again, we have a responsibility to respond properly to this pruning process. We must remain humble and teachable, patiently enduring the process so that we can receive the good benefit that will come from the pruning.

Vi's Gardening Tip:

How should we respond in times of pruning? Here are some tips to help you endure the pruning process:

- Stay rooted in knowing that Christ loves you perfectly. (Remember our lesson on being rooted in His love.) Remember that He is pruning you because He loves and cares for you. Watch out for bitter roots during these times. Don't grumble, complain, or get angry.

- Remember that the pruning is for your ultimate good and growth, even though for a while it may really hurt. Trust and believe that God is using it to create even more life in you. Meditate on Scriptures that encourage you to hope in God's unfailing love and goodness. (Lamentations 3:32 says, "Though he brings grief, he will show compassion, so great is his unfailing love.")

- Stay humble and teachable, carefully examining your garden for any weed or other distractions that your Master Gardener is trying to remove.

- Be quick to confess any sin (1 John 1:9). Repent of (or turn away from) these things.

- Maintain an attitude of thanksgiving and hope (James 1:2-4), setting your eyes on the hope of a more lush and fruitful garden yet to come.

Sweet flowers are slow and weeds make haste.
—William Shakespeare

Lesson Twenty

Oaks of Righteousness

Don't you love trees? Have you ever seen a large, majestic tree standing proud and upright in the middle of a field? It stands faithfully rooted, immovable, and steadfast. It provides fruit, shelter, and shade for men and animals. It even offers a jungle gym to the young. The shaggy girth of its trunk provides a place for people to carve their initials. Its leafy arms are raised to the heavens in praise. Its branches sway gracefully in the breeze as if worshipping its Creator.

Joy

Psalm 96:12-13 declares, "Let the fields be jubilant, and everything in them. Then all the trees of the forest will sing for joy; they will sing before the LORD, for he comes." Can you picture this in your mind? What a wonderful description of creation rejoicing in the coming of Jesus—who will establish righteousness in the new heaven and new earth! But it's fun to imagine that the trees are praising God even now!

Did you know that the Bible says you are like a tree? The Lord makes the comparison between the life of those redeemed by God and an oak tree. Look up Isaiah 61:3 and write it below:

This is the fruit of having the life of Christ growing in you—you will become an "oak of righteousness." To be "righteous" simply means to be right with God. We are made right with God—righteous—through our relationship with Christ.

Use your imagination: What are some characteristics of a mighty oak tree—characteristics you also possess in Christ? Write your thoughts below:

As you read the next three Scripture passages in this lesson, get out your colored pencils and identify some key words. Draw a brown tree around any references to trees. Draw a red apple around any references to fruit. Draw green leaves around any references to leaves. Draw blue water drops for any mention of water and use black for roots. Finally, draw purple flowers to identify any blessings mentioned in the passages.

> BUT BLESSED IS THE MAN WHO TRUSTS IN THE LORD, WHOSE CONFIDENCE IS IN HIM. HE WILL BE LIKE A TREE PLANTED BY THE WATER THAT SENDS OUT ITS ROOTS BY THE STREAM. IT DOES NOT FEAR WHEN HEAT COMES; ITS LEAVES ARE ALWAYS GREEN. IT HAS NO WORRIES IN A YEAR OF DROUGHT AND NEVER FAILS TO BEAR FRUIT. —JEREMIAH 17:7-8

The righteous man in this passage has his roots anchored deeply in the love of God—meaning he trusts the Lord. (Remember Lesson 15—Rooted in Christ.)

Let's look at another illustration from Psalm 1:1-6 that beautifully depicts the believer's life as a tree. Don't forget your colored pencils!

BLESSED IS THE MAN WHO DOES NOT WALK IN THE COUNSEL OF THE WICKED OR STAND IN THE WAY OF SINNERS OR SIT IN THE SEAT OF MOCKERS. BUT HIS DELIGHT IS IN THE LAW OF THE LORD, AND ON HIS LAW HE MEDITATES DAY AND NIGHT. HE IS LIKE A TREE PLANTED BY STREAMS OF WATER, WHICH YIELDS ITS FRUIT IN SEASON AND WHOSE LEAF DOES NOT WITHER. WHATEVER HE DOES PROSPERS.

NOT SO THE WICKED! THEY ARE LIKE CHAFF THAT THE WIND BLOWS AWAY. THEREFORE THE WICKED WILL NOT STAND IN THE JUDGMENT, NOR SINNERS IN THE ASSEMBLY OF THE RIGHTEOUS.

FOR THE LORD WATCHES OVER THE WAY OF THE RIGHTEOUS, BUT THE WAY OF THE WICKED WILL PERISH. —PSALM 1:1-6

The analogy of our lives in Christ as strong, healthy trees is so inspiring. Challenge yourself to memorize Psalm 1 in its entirety. Consider writing it out on a fancy or colorful sheet of paper and hanging it on your bathroom mirror, where you can reflect on its beautiful meaning each morning.

Now let's study one last passage from Psalm 92:12-14 to allow this truth to take root in our hearts:

THE RIGHTEOUS WILL FLOURISH LIKE A PALM TREE, THEY WILL GROW LIKE A CEDAR OF LEBANON; PLANTED IN THE HOUSE OF THE LORD, THEY WILL FLOURISH IN THE COURTS OF OUR GOD. THEY WILL STILL BEAR FRUIT IN OLD AGE, THEY WILL STAY FRESH AND GREEN. —PSALM 92:12-14

The cedars of Lebanon were of great importance to the ancient people. The wood was so valuable that King Solomon used these magnificent trees to build his palace and the temple in Jerusalem. Cedars of Lebanon are a deep, rich red color and are quite aromatic. The wood is strong and solid with very few knots. They grow well over 100 feet in height. Cedars of Lebanon symbolize strength and magnificence. To find out more about the cedars of Lebanon, refer to Section 5 in the Appendix.

Reflection:

Based on what you now know about the cedars of Lebanon, re-read Psalm 92:12-14. What does the phrase "they will grow like a cedar of Lebanon" mean to you now?

Look over the two passages (Psalm 1:1-6 and Psalm 92:12-14) and list every blessing you circled in purple. We'll get you started:

- He is confident and secure.
- He will not fear when the heat of the trials and pressures of life come.
- He drinks deeply from God's river, never thirsty.

Just look at all of the wonderful blessings that can be yours as the life of Christ grows within the garden of your heart!

Vi's Gardening Tip:

Always remember that this is what you are—an oak of righteousness, a cedar of Lebanon, a planting of the Lord! This is God's amazing plan for your life. You will be strong and magnificent and valuable to God because of the quality and strength of character inside of you, which is the life of Christ growing within. God's desire is for you to flourish and grow and bear fruit even in old age. What a beautiful illustration of the fruitfulness of our lives and our usefulness to God if we allow the life of Christ to take root in our hearts. Never forget!

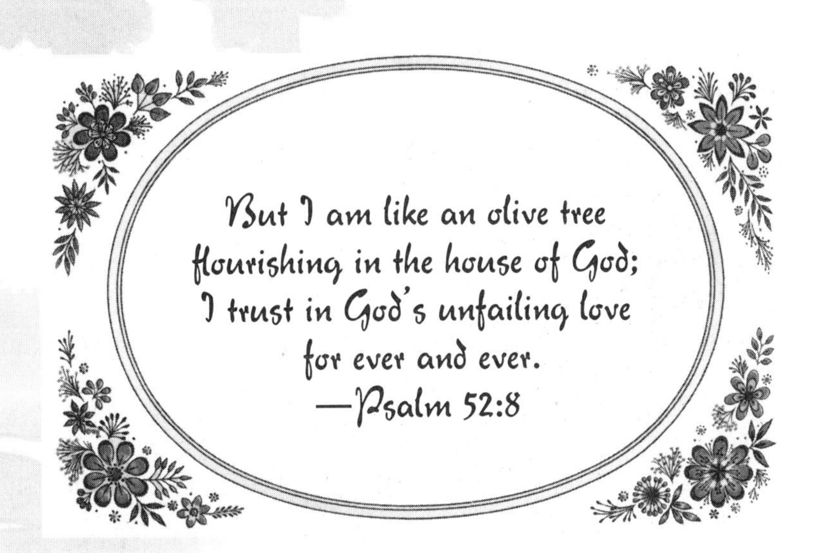

But I am like an olive tree
flourishing in the house of God;
I trust in God's unfailing love
for ever and ever.
—Psalm 52:8

Lesson Twenty-One

A Well-Watered Garden

We all know how important water is for plants and trees to grow and survive. Humans are no different. Our bodies need physical water—and so do our souls. God desires the garden of your heart to always be watered and refreshed, even if you are going through a spiritually dry time or a very difficult trial.

Read the promises found in Isaiah 58:11. Underline every promise you can find:

> The Lord will guide you always; he will satisfy your needs in a sun-scorched land and will strengthen your frame. You will be like a well-watered garden, like a spring whose waters never fail. —Isaiah 58:11

Your loving Master Gardener has planned for you to have an endless, eternal supply of His thirst-quenching and life-giving water. He has provided an ever-lasting, ever-bubbling fountain of water for your garden. Let's look closely again at the beautiful Garden of Eden in the second chapter of Genesis. The following passages describe how God watered this magnificent garden. Using a blue pencil, underline every reference to water. Draw blue water drops over the names of the four headwaters mentioned in verses 10-14:

> ... AND NO SHRUB OF THE FIELD HAD YET APPEARED ON THE EARTH AND NO PLANT OF THE FIELD HAD YET SPRUNG UP, FOR THE LORD GOD HAD NOT SENT RAIN ON THE EARTH AND THERE WAS NO MAN TO WORK THE GROUND, BUT STREAMS CAME UP FROM THE EARTH AND WATERED THE WHOLE SURFACE OF THE GROUND. —GENESIS 2:5-6

> A RIVER WATERING THE GARDEN FLOWED FROM EDEN; FROM THERE IT WAS SEPARATED INTO FOUR HEADWATERS. THE NAME OF THE FIRST IS THE PISHON; IT WINDS THROUGH THE ENTIRE LAND OF HAVILAH, WHERE THERE IS GOLD. (THE GOLD OF THAT LAND IS GOOD; AROMATIC RESIN AND ONYX ARE ALSO THERE.) THE NAME OF THE SECOND RIVER IS THE GIHON; IT WINDS THROUGH THE ENTIRE LAND OF CUSH. THE NAME OF THE THIRD RIVER IS THE TIGRIS; IT RUNS ALONG THE EAST SIDE OF ASSHUR. AND THE FOURTH RIVER IS THE EUPHRATES. —GENESIS 2:10-14

Imagine how beautiful these four rivers must have been—powerful torrents of water cascading over rocks and falls. Instead of rain, there were streams and possibly fine, refreshing mists coming up from the earth to water the surface like a sprinkler system you might have in your own yard, only without the hose.

Read the following Scriptures and draw blue water drops over all the places that speak of water. You might want to use a blue pencil and use raindrops or something creative to mark your water passages.

Psalm 36:8-9

They feast on the abundance of your house; you give them drink from your river of delights. For with you is the fountain of life; in your light we see light.

Isaiah 12:2-3

Surely God is my salvation; I will trust and not be afraid. The Lord, the Lord, is my strength and my song; he has become my salvation. With joy you will draw water from the wells of salvation.

John 7:37-38

On the last and greatest day of the Feast, Jesus stood and said in a loud voice, "If anyone is thirsty, let him come to me and drink. Whoever believes in me, as the Scripture has said, streams of living water will flow from within him."

John 4:14

But whoever drinks the water I give him will never thirst. Indeed, the water I give him will become in him a spring of water welling up to eternal life.

REFLECTION:

1. Who is the supplier of water for your garden?

2. List the different water sources mentioned in the earlier verses:

These are all pictures of what Christ is to us. He is our source of living water. He is the river, the fountain, the well, the spring, or the stream in your garden. How wonderful to sit by running, bubbling water! Doesn't it refresh your soul and relax you as you listen to its cheery tune running onward with joy and delight, never tiring, never ceasing? This is always available for you through Christ, your Fountain of Living Water. Anytime you feel tired, stressed, or thirsty, go to Him, your garden of communion, and drink in the comfort and refreshment only He can bring.

Jesus claims to be your never-ending supply of water. Look at the passages from John. What did He say would happen to you if you would drink regularly from Him? Write your thoughts below:

God promises to make YOU a fountain of living water for others! Your garden was meant to be a fruitful place that will bless not only the Lord but also those around you. You can be a refreshing source of water that spills into another's dry, parched garden. How wonderful it is to be a vessel of living water that receives life from Christ and flows forth into the world!

John, in his book of Revelation, was given a glimpse into heavenly realms. Read what he saw when he looked into Heaven:

> THEN THE ANGEL SHOWED ME THE RIVER OF THE WATER OF LIFE, AS CLEAR AS CRYSTAL, FLOWING FROM THE THRONE OF GOD AND OF THE LAMB.
>
> —REVELATION 22:1

This river is not just awaiting you in Heaven. It is gushing forth for you now. It is a mighty river flowing from the very throne of God. Christ, God's Son, is pouring out His life for you and for a very thirsty, dry, and weary world.

Vi's Gardening Tip:

Will you drink from Christ so you will never thirst again? Will you drink so that others can be refreshed through you? In Matthew 11:28, Jesus says, "Come to me, all you who are weary and burdened, and I will give you rest." Go to Christ and you too will sing with those who are drinking from this River of Life. "As they make music they will sing, 'All my fountains are in you' " (Psalm 87:7).

Gardening requires lots of water—most of it in the form of perspiration.
—Lou Erickson

Lesson Twenty-Two

Sun for the Garden

Just as plants and gardens need water to thrive and grow, they also need light. Take a plant into a dark closet and it will soon die. So it is with your spiritual life. The garden of your soul needs light in order to flourish and survive.

Read the following passage slowly. Draw a yellow sun over the word "light."

> And God said, "Let there be light," and there was light. God saw that the light was good, and he separated the light from the darkness. God called the light "day," and the darkness he called "night." And there was evening, and there was morning—the first day. —Genesis 1:3-5

From the very beginning of creation, we see that God created light. He called it "good" and He separated it from darkness. Here we see that God is making a distinction between light and darkness. There are two realms, two kingdoms: the kingdom of light and the kingdom of darkness.

First let's talk about light. Read the following verses slowly. Then go back and draw a yellow sun over the word "light." Next, draw a pink flower over the word "life." Connect the two words in each verse when you can.

THE LORD IS MY LIGHT AND MY SALVATION. —PSALM 27:1

FOR WITH YOU IS THE FOUNTAIN OF LIFE; IN YOUR LIGHT WE SEE LIGHT. —PSALM 36:9

IN HIM WAS LIFE, AND THAT LIFE WAS THE LIGHT OF MEN. THE LIGHT SHINES IN THE DARKNESS, BUT THE DARKNESS HAS NOT UNDERSTOOD IT. —JOHN 1:4-5

I AM THE LIGHT OF THE WORLD. WHOEVER FOLLOWS ME WILL NEVER WALK IN DARKNESS, BUT WILL HAVE THE LIGHT OF LIFE. —JOHN 8:12

There is absolutely no darkness in God or in His Kingdom. God is pure light, and pure light is perfection—pure holiness. Christ is God's light sent into this world of darkness (John 8:12). Jesus is the only source of spiritual light. In His light, we find life. You can't have spiritual life without the light of Christ. He is the sun shining on your garden. Where His light shines, there will be unending abundant life and growth. Anything good, pure, holy, right, and lovely springs up from under the light of Christ.

Satan, on the other hand, is the lord of the kingdom of darkness. Anything wicked, evil, and unrighteous lurks in the kingdom of darkness. There is no life in the kingdom of darkness.

Carefully read the following Scriptures below. Once again, draw a yellow sun over the word "light" and underline the words "dark/darkness" in black. Then answer the questions following.

> For you were once darkness, but now you are light in the Lord. Live as children of light (for the fruit of the light consists in all goodness, righteousness and truth) and find out what pleases the Lord. Have nothing to do with the fruitless deeds of darkness, but rather expose them. For it is shameful even to mention what the disobedient do in secret. But everything exposed by the light becomes visible, for it is light that makes everything visible. This is why it is said: "Wake up, O sleeper, rise from the dead, and Christ will shine on you." —Ephesians 5:8-14

> This is the verdict: Light has come into the world, but men loved darkness instead of light because their deeds were evil. Everyone who does evil hates the light, and will not come into the light for fear that his deeds will be exposed. But whoever lives by the truth comes into the light, so that it may be seen plainly that what he has done has been done through God. —John 3:19-21

Describe the fruit of the light:

Is there any good fruit found in darkness? What are the deeds of darkness?

What does the light do?

As children of light, what is our responsibility in regard to darkness and the evil hiding there?

From reading these passages, we learn some very important spiritual principles that we must know in order to keep our garden growing strong and healthy. First, we see that light makes things visible. It exposes and reveals things for what they are; they are either from the kingdom of light or from the kingdom of darkness. Those who love truth walk in the light.

As we mentioned earlier, the kingdom of darkness breeds every evil and wicked thing. Those who love wickedness hate the light, because their evil deeds will be exposed. Therefore they long to hide in the covering of darkness. Any thoughts or deeds that remain hidden in the darkness are under the power of the evil one.

If you have Christ living in you, you are a child of the light. You must live in the light (the truth) and you must have nothing to do with the kingdom of darkness. In fact, as we read above, we are to be diligent to watch over our garden for any darkness and bring it immediately into the light. If it stays in the darkness, Satan has power over it and will use it against you.

Let's read another passage that helps us understand even more why we must be diligent garden watchmen who walk in the light. Again, with your colored pencils, be on the lookout for the words "light" and "darkness."

> [5]THIS IS THE MESSAGE WE HAVE HEARD FROM HIM AND DECLARE TO YOU: GOD IS LIGHT; IN HIM THERE IS NO DARKNESS AT ALL. [6]IF WE CLAIM TO HAVE FELLOWSHIP WITH HIM YET WALK IN THE DARKNESS, WE LIE AND DO NOT LIVE BY THE TRUTH. [7]BUT IF WE WALK IN THE LIGHT, AS HE IS IN THE LIGHT, WE HAVE FELLOWSHIP WITH ONE ANOTHER, AND THE BLOOD OF

JESUS, HIS SON, PURIFIES US FROM ALL SIN. [8]IF WE CLAIM TO BE WITHOUT SIN, WE DECEIVE OURSELVES AND THE TRUTH IS NOT IN US. [9]IF WE CONFESS OUR SINS, HE IS FAITHFUL AND JUST AND WILL FORGIVE US OUR SINS AND PURIFY US FROM ALL UNRIGHTEOUSNESS. —1 JOHN 1:5-9

You are a child of light and you must know how to walk in the light. Christ wants to shine His light on all the dark crevices of your garden so there is no evil thing growing there. Remember, light exposes that which is hidden in darkness. The light of Christ's presence, the Holy Spirit within, will show you areas of sin that may be lurking under a rock or hiding in the shadows. When you feel the gentle nudge of the Holy Spirit directing you to an area of darkness in your garden, you must choose to bring it into the light and be honest about it with God and with others. You must confess the sin and ask the Master Gardener to remove it far from you. To *confess* means to agree with God and to acknowledge your sin. You are saying to God, "Yes, Lord, I sinned when I lied to my mother. I see my sin and I'm sorry. I want You to get it out of my garden!" An amazing thing happens when we do this; the light of Christ will act as a laser to extinguish this area of darkness. We are immediately forgiven and purified, and our fellowship with God and others in our life is restored (verses 7 and 9).

List any areas of darkness lurking in your garden that the Holy Spirit has revealed to you.

Refusing to repent from your sins when the Holy Spirit convicts you is what verse 6 refers to as "walking in the darkness." If we choose to love the darkness and keep our sins hidden in our gardens, then we will damage our fellowship with God and with others. Our beautiful plants will wilt and die. Ugly, wicked things will grow instead.

There are other things besides sin that hide in the darkness. Our thoughts and feelings may also need to be exposed to the light. Feelings such as fear, guilt, doubt, condemnation, or even troubling events from your past need to be talked about and exposed to the light of God's truth. In the book *Violet's Hidden Doubts*, our own dear Vi learned the importance of bringing fears and doubts into the light. When she finally opened her heart to her mother about her own dark thoughts, God was then able to show her the lies Satan had planted in her mind. She immediately felt free of the feelings of depression, guilt, and fear, and God's joy and peace once again flooded back into her soul. Sometimes, as with Vi, this can be a quick process, but sometimes God will set you free by taking you on a journey. Trust Him for His perfect timing.

Reflection:

Are there any areas of darkness hiding in your garden (like fear or doubts) which you have not brought into the light? Search not only your actions, but your thoughts and feelings as well. Write them below. Then confess them to the Lord.

Consider being open and honest with a trusted adult, a parent, a mentor, or a pastor about these areas of darkness. They can pray for you and help you bring God's truth into your situation. Keep your garden bathed in the holy, cleansing light of God, and life will abound!

Vi's Gardening Tip:

If you want good, holy plants growing in your garden, you must love the light and be willing to let Christ show you things, even when you don't want to see them. It's not easy to look at our sins. We feel ashamed and embarrassed, or sometimes we don't want to get rid of the sin because we like it. It's sometimes scary to be honest and vulnerable with others when it comes to our fears and doubts. But we must look fully into the sunshine. It's the only way to really live! As a sunflower lifts its face to the sun, lift your soul to the Son and let His light bathe your garden with life.

The sun, with all those planets revolving around it and dependent on it,
can still ripen a bunch of grapes as if it had nothing else in the universe to do.
—Galileo

Lesson Twenty-Three

Storms

Storms will blow against your garden. This happens in nature and in our spiritual lives also. Christ is our heavenly sunshine and His light is always there for us, but sometimes the clouds of life block the sun so we can't see it. Have you ever flown on an airplane when it was very cloudy at takeoff? When the plane reaches a high enough altitude to break above the clouds, suddenly you see the sun shining in all its glory! The sun was always shining in full strength, but you couldn't see it for the clouds. We must remember this when our gardens are being pelted by the wind and rain of the storms of life. The warmth of God's love and care is there; you just can't see it in that moment.

God allows the storms to blow against your garden for a very important reason. He uses the storms to keep the soil in your garden soft. The soil in our hearts easily becomes hardened and packed down by pride and self-righteousness. We all have those places at one time or another throughout our spiritual growth. God understands our nature and lovingly comes to help keep our hearts soft. Storms come in the way of trials, hardships, and sufferings. Tears of suffering and sorrow fall like rain and soften dry, parched ground. The strong winds of adversity beat and blow against our gardens with such force that our plants seem to bend so low as to break. But in this place of weakness, as we are bowed down, we learn humility and trust in God.

Sometimes it may not be the hardened places of pride and self-righteousness that God wants to reach, but maybe there are places in our hearts that have been untouched and God wants to ready that area for new growth. For instance, perhaps you are unaware of the needs of the elderly. But then a "storm" hits your family. Your grandfather has a stroke and must be cared for in a nursing home. Because of this storm, your heart is now sensitive and aware of the sufferings of the elderly. You become a regular visitor to that nursing home, bringing joy and hope to the lonely residents.

Whatever the situation, our attitude in response to the storms God sends is important. When we KNOW that God is good, we can trust Him in all things. We can respond to trials and hardships with positive attitudes of faith and thanksgiving.

Reflection:

What concerns you the most about the thought of God using hardship and suffering to cultivate the soil of your heart?

Why do you think hardships soften us toward the ways of God?

What Scriptures do you share (or words of encouragement do you say) to comfort a friend who is suffering a trial? Write them in the space below and refer to them when you yourself are suffering a storm of life. You can refer to the "Seeds for Your Storms" card in the Seed Packets of Truth section of the Appendix for ideas.

If you have been through a hard trial, write down how it helped you to grow toward God. What did you learn about God through the suffering? What did you learn about yourself? Did it change the way you relate to others in need? Write your reflections below:

Let's look at some things you can do to help weather life's storms. As you read through the following text, underline anything that stands out to you:

First, stay rooted in God's love. Refer to Lesson 15: "Rooted in Christ." When you are rooted in the knowledge of God's love, you can stand firm against the winds of adversity. During times of testing or hardship, your enemy, Satan, will speak lies and tell you that God doesn't love you, that He is angry with you, that He is disappointed with you, or that He has abandoned you. Despite this opposition to your faith, you must stand strong and declare, "God loves me!" Stay secure in knowing that He promises to never leave you (Hebrews 13:5).

Next, understand that all storms eventually pass. Psalm 30:5 says, "Weeping may remain for a night, but rejoicing comes in the morning." Storms come and go. They never stay. Remember this when the night is dark and you can't see the sun and you feel like it will never end. It will; it must. Morning always comes. The sun will return and you will once again rejoice.

Trust your Lord and hold tight to Him. He will get you through. John 16:33 says, "I have told you these things, so that in me you may have peace. In this world you will have trouble. But take heart! I have overcome the world." Jesus was honest with us about troubles—storms—in our lives. He warned us to expect them, but in the same breath He informed us to be encouraged and to "take heart." Jesus is greater than any storm that will come against your garden!

James 1:2-4 tells us to consider it joy when the trials come:

Joy

CONSIDER IT PURE JOY, MY BROTHERS, WHENEVER YOU FACE TRIALS OF MANY KINDS, BECAUSE YOU KNOW THAT THE TESTING OF YOUR FAITH DEVELOPS PERSEVERANCE. PERSEVERANCE MUST FINISH ITS WORK SO THAT YOU MAY BE MATURE AND COMPLETE, NOT LACKING ANYTHING. —JAMES 1:2-4

You don't have to be joyful about the trials, but you can be joyful about the good fruit they will produce in your heart. A great harvest of righteousness will come to you on the other side of a storm, so you can start being thankful for it ahead of time! We must see the situation the way God sees it. He's not out to harm us. He's looking ahead at the beautiful fruit and flowers that will come after the storm.

Look again at James 1:2-4 above, and review the following two Scriptures below. In each, underline the "fruit" that is produced after going through a storm:

NOT ONLY SO, BUT WE ALSO REJOICE IN OUR SUFFERINGS, BECAUSE WE KNOW THAT SUFFERING PRODUCES PERSEVERANCE, PERSEVERANCE; CHARACTER; AND CHARACTER, HOPE. —ROMANS 5:3-4

AND THE GOD OF ALL GRACE, WHO CALLED YOU TO HIS ETERNAL GLORY IN CHRIST, AFTER YOU HAVE SUFFERED A LITTLE WHILE, WILL HIMSELF RESTORE YOU AND MAKE YOU STRONG, FIRM AND STEADFAST. —1 PETER 5:10

Wow! That's a lot of good fruit! Storms serve to strengthen you, not to break you. You must have the stormy days to enjoy the sunny days. "April showers bring May flowers." If you want flowers in your garden, then embrace the storms. You can't have one without the other. After the storm passes, there is such a sweet, serene calm. The air is fresher, the grass is greener than ever, and the flowers are more brilliant in color. The storm has served a great purpose for your garden.

SEE! THE WINTER IS PAST; THE RAINS ARE OVER AND GONE. FLOWERS APPEAR ON THE EARTH; THE SEASON OF SINGING HAS COME, THE COOING OF DOVES IS HEARD IN OUR LAND. —SONG OF SONGS 2:11-12

Vi's Gardening Tip:

In a journal or on a separate sheet of paper, consider listing the benefits of storms that you have learned in this lesson. You could even make a collage of Scriptures and/or pictures to encourage you on those stormy days.

Be thou the rainbow in the storms of life. The evening beam that smiles the clouds away, and tints tomorrow with prophetic ray.
—Lord Byron

Lesson Twenty-Four

YOUR WILDERNESS WILL BLOOM!

In case you're experiencing doubts that even God's thumb is truly green enough to transform your weedy and barren garden into a lush and fruitful harvest of righteousness, let this lesson bring hope and encouragement. Your Master Gardener is able to do the miraculous for your garden—to make something from nothing.

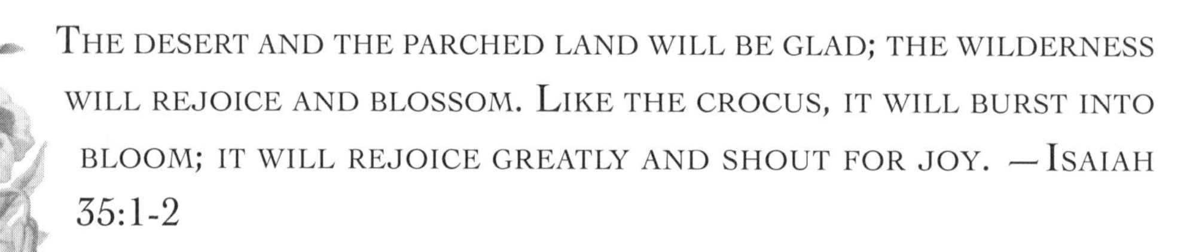

THE DESERT AND THE PARCHED LAND WILL BE GLAD; THE WILDERNESS WILL REJOICE AND BLOSSOM. LIKE THE CROCUS, IT WILL BURST INTO BLOOM; IT WILL REJOICE GREATLY AND SHOUT FOR JOY. —ISAIAH 35:1-2

Joy

(Refer to Section 4: "Flowers of the Bible" in the Appendix for more information on the saffron crocus.)

God is the Creator of all life. "In the beginning God created the heavens and the earth," says Genesis 1:1. He is life itself. He delights in taking that which is dead, barren, and desolate and creating lush, fertile, and fruitful life: "Now the earth was formless and empty, darkness was over the surface of the deep, and the Spirit of God was hovering over the waters. And God said—" (Genesis 1:2-3).

Now that's *some* kind of gardener, wouldn't you say? With a word, God created life upon the earth, which was formless and empty. With this as our reference as to what God can do with nothing, surely you can believe that God can do something with you! God can take your life and speak living words into the empty, lonely, and hurting places of your soul and create newness. He can turn your failures around, and He most certainly forgives your sins.

There is no place for despair and hopelessness with God. He never sees failure. He never sees loss. He doesn't even see death. He always sees His purposes, His plans, and His desires for us, all of which are full of His life. He is the amazing Redeemer and Restorer of our souls. *He sees the potential of your garden.*

Look carefully at the incredible hope given to us in Isaiah 41:18-20:

> I WILL MAKE RIVERS FLOW ON BARREN HEIGHTS, AND SPRINGS WITHIN THE VALLEYS. I WILL TURN THE DESERT INTO POOLS OF WATER, AND THE PARCHED GROUND INTO SPRINGS. I WILL PUT IN THE DESERT THE CEDAR AND THE ACACIA, THE MYRTLE AND THE OLIVE. I WILL SET PINES IN THE WASTELAND, THE FIR AND THE CYPRESS TOGETHER, SO THAT PEOPLE MAY SEE AND KNOW, MAY CONSIDER AND UNDERSTAND, THAT THE HAND OF THE LORD HAS DONE THIS, THAT THE HOLY ONE OF ISRAEL HAS CREATED IT. —ISAIAH 41:18-20

Using the above Scripture verses, fill in the following chart to show the transformation of the land after God spoke life over it.

BEFORE	AFTER
Barren Heights	
Valleys	

Deserts	
Parched Ground	
Wasteland	

To learn more about the different variety of plants from the Isaiah passage, refer to Section 5: "Trees of the Bible" in the Appendix.

Reflection:

These desert and barren places can represent wilderness times—past or present— in your life, such as experiencing a divorce in your family, moving to a new place and feeling lonely, the death of a loved one, or suffering with an illness. We all experience these barren places at different times in our lives. They come and go like the seasons.

1. What barren "wilderness" time are you going through now? (It could be something as small as struggling through math class or as large as mourning the loss of a loved one.) Describe it below:

2. Refer to your Seed Packets of Truth cards and choose a Scripture that you can "sow" into your barren ground. Write it below. Water this seed through faith and believe in the harvest to come.

3. Finally, what beautiful, blooming promise can you see coming forth from this seed of truth?

Only the green thumb of your Master Gardener can create life in a wilderness. He will do this in your garden also. It is through Christ's amazing life, sacrificial death, and resurrection that we are able to bloom. Christ can take our pain, sorrow, failure, and losses and turn them into fruitful places. He will take those seasons of suffering (the wilderness of our souls) and cause a harvest to spring forth—a harvest that will glorify God and cause our lives to be a comfort and a blessing to others. We only need to allow Christ's love and life to grow within us.

Vi's Gardening Tip:

Make a blooming collage of hope to remind you that God's seed of truth will bloom in your barren place. Write the Scripture from your reflection question in the center of a piece of construction paper. Decorate the rest of the page with cutouts of flowers, fruits, and trees. Put the artwork in a place where you will see it regularly. Be thankful and have faith that in due season your wilderness will bloom with joy.

. . . and provide for those who grieve in Zion— to bestow on them a crown of beauty instead of ashes, the oil of gladness instead of mourning, and a garment of praise instead of a spirit of despair. They will be called oaks of righteousness, a planting of the LORD for the display of his splendor.
—Isaiah 61:3

The Invitation...

Imagine sitting under a gently swaying cypress tree or shady oak tree in the garden of your heart. You are surrounded by fragrant, colorful blossoms, hearty vines, and ripening fruit. Side by side you have labored with the Master Gardener to cultivate your life of faith, and you are beginning to see the fruits of your labor. You are overjoyed at how your faith has grown and matured. You realize that your relationship with God is stronger, more deeply rooted. It has not been easy, but you have persevered, and your garden continues to grow toward Heaven.

As you take in the serenity of your garden, you hear something in the distance. A sound is coming from beyond your garden wall. You recognize it—yes! It is the voice of the Master Gardener, and He is beckoning you to step outside of your garden to join Him in a different kind of work. He calls on you, for He knows that you are now ready to share your experiences and faith with others.

Unable to resist His call, you slowly venture through your garden gate. What you see before you is astounding! Stretched out as far as your eye can see is a great harvest field, only there is not wheat or corn to gather in, but people—people of every age and race and from every country around the world! It is God's great harvest field, and He has invited you to help Him labor in these amazing pastures. Your heart beats wildly inside your chest. Somehow you know that you were always destined to be a part of this work. You look up into the Master Gardener's eyes, and suddenly you see Him in a different light. He is now Lord of the Harvest, and you stand in awe of Him. With great compassion and fire in His eyes, He hands you a special plow and begins to share His heart for the lost with you:

"As you can see, my child, there is a bountiful harvest, but not enough workers. Will you be a worker in my harvest fields? Each soul is precious to me. I desire for each one of them to have his or her own garden of fellowship with me through my Son, just as you and I share."

His words ring within your soul. You take the plow in hand and know that this may be the biggest challenge of your life, but you also know that you cannot turn away, for the Lord's desire is now burning within your own heart. Somehow you understand that this will be the most joyful and satisfying work you have ever done. And you know that you will never be alone. You look out across the fields once again and into the eyes of the souls waiting there. With God at your side and His love in your heart, you bravely step forward. Your life can now become fruit and refreshment to these hungering souls, and the Lord of the Harvest could not be more pleased.

Lesson Twenty-Five

Harvesting with the Lord

What joy to labor side by side with the Lord of the Harvest in His great field of souls! The work you did in your own heart's garden has prepared you to share the love of Christ with others. Nothing could be more exciting or satisfying. We were each created to worship and love God, and then to share His message with others.

Just as the great Lord of the Harvest gathered your soul into His Kingdom, He desires for every person to enter His eternal gates. Each soul is invaluable to the Lord. He overlooks no one. As you begin this new adventure of harvesting with the Lord, there are some very important principles that you must understand. God's unending love for the lost is the first one.

Read the following parables from Luke 15:4-10. Using a vibrant orange pencil, draw a heart around the words "joyfully" and "rejoice."

> SUPPOSE ONE OF YOU HAS A HUNDRED SHEEP AND LOSES ONE OF THEM. DOES HE NOT LEAVE THE NINETY-NINE IN THE OPEN COUNTRY AND GO AFTER THE LOST SHEEP UNTIL HE FINDS IT? AND WHEN HE FINDS IT, HE JOYFULLY

PUTS IT ON HIS SHOULDERS AND GOES HOME. THEN HE CALLS HIS FRIENDS AND NEIGHBORS TOGETHER AND SAYS, "REJOICE WITH ME; I HAVE FOUND MY LOST SHEEP." I TELL YOU THAT IN THE SAME WAY THERE WILL BE MORE REJOICING IN HEAVEN OVER ONE SINNER WHO REPENTS THAN OVER NINETY-NINE RIGHTEOUS PERSONS WHO DO NOT NEED TO REPENT. OR SUPPOSE A WOMAN HAS TEN SILVER COINS AND LOSES ONE. DOES SHE NOT LIGHT A LAMP, SWEEP THE HOUSE AND SEARCH CAREFULLY UNTIL SHE FINDS IT? AND WHEN SHE FINDS IT, SHE CALLS HER FRIENDS AND NEIGHBORS TOGETHER AND SAYS, "REJOICE WITH ME; I HAVE FOUND MY LOST COIN." IN THE SAME WAY, I TELL YOU, THERE IS REJOICING IN THE PRESENCE OF THE ANGELS OF GOD OVER ONE SINNER WHO REPENTS.—LUKE 15:4-10

Now go back and circle the word "one" in the passage above. What does this passage show you about the heart of the Lord of the Harvest? Write your thoughts below:

In these parables, the Lord of the Harvest is attempting to describe to us how great His joy is when a lost soul finds Christ. He longs for us to share in His intense joy. Joy is not complete until someone shares it with you. The Lord of the Harvest invites us to be participants of the joy of His great harvest of souls. He wants His joy to spill onto us and splash out onto others.

As our love and faith grow and mature in Christ, our focus turns less to self and more toward others. We begin to share God's heart for those who are lost and hurting. We begin to grieve over the things He grieves over and rejoice when He rejoices. This is part of our growing and maturing process. It is the fullness of the Seed of Christ bearing fruit in our lives. At this place of growth we are ready to partner with the Lord in the great work of harvesting souls.

Reflection:

1. Have you given much thought to soul-harvesting up until now? Write your thoughts below:

2. How do you imagine yourself helping God to "harvest" souls? (There is no right or wrong answer.)

To *harvest* means to gather in. There is a great ingathering of souls into God's Kingdom that happens every single minute of every day. Who are the people God is gathering into His Kingdom? They are people of all ages from every nation, tribe, and tongue around the world. Think for a moment about the people in your life—family members, friends, acquaintances, etc. Imagine their faces. They are part of God's harvest fields! Does one person stand out in your mind? Jot his or her name down and begin to pray that soul into God's Kingdom.

____

In the natural world, the harvest is a time of gathering in the crops and enjoying the fruit of much labor. Harvest time has always been an occasion for great rejoicing throughout the ages. The Israelites celebrated several feasts and festivals during their harvest times. (Read more about the "Feast of the Firstfruits" in Section 3 of the Appendix.) Feasting, dancing, and singing were a big part of the harvest celebration. Likewise, there is much rejoicing and singing in Heaven when even a single soul is harvested and brought into the Kingdom of God.

Imagine the celestial singing and unending joy going on in Heaven because of the great harvest of all the regions around the world! This song of the harvest is going out across Heaven and earth; it is the song of victory and triumph—a song of the redeemed, purchased by the blood of the Lamb of God—Christ, your Spiritual Seed. If only we could put on supernatural headphones and listen to this never-ending, heavenly symphony!

Read the following verses from Revelation 5:9-10:

> And they sang a new song, saying: "You are worthy to take the scroll, and to open its seals; for You were slain, and have redeemed us to God by Your blood out of every tribe and tongue and people and nation, and have made us kings and priests to our God; and we shall reign on the earth."—Revelation 5:9-10 (New King James Version)

From what part of the earth does this song of victory rise?

The Lord of the Harvest wants us to experience the greatest thrill of all—seeing a life transformed from darkness into His marvelous light. He wants us to partner with Him in this miracle. The Lord of the Harvest is singing the song of the Harvest. Will you sing with Him? Will you offer yourself and enter into the joy of the Lord?

> His master replied, "Well done, good and faithful servant! You have been faithful with a few things; I will put you in charge of many things. Come and share your master's happiness!" —Matthew 25:21

Vi's Gardening Tip:

Having a heart for the lost may not come easily or naturally for you. Do not be distressed! Pray and ask the Lord of the Harvest to begin to soften your heart for the lost souls of the world. As you grow more in the likeness of Christ, you will grow to love the lost, too.

The highest reward for a person's toil is not what they get for it, but what they become by it.
—John Ruskin

Lesson Twenty-Six

The Call of the Harvest

In our study we have seen how Jesus has been at the center of the garden of our hearts. It is His seed growing within our lives that brings forth the joy, fruit, and maturity we long for. It should be no surprise, then, to know that Jesus is at the center of the great harvest! Let's look at the last words of Jesus before He returned to His Father in Heaven. This passage of Scripture is known as the Great Commission, but we shall call it the *Great Harvest Invitation:*

> ALL AUTHORITY IN HEAVEN AND ON EARTH HAS BEEN GIVEN TO ME. THEREFORE GO AND MAKE DISCIPLES OF ALL NATIONS, BAPTIZING THEM IN THE NAME OF THE FATHER AND OF THE SON AND OF THE HOLY SPIRIT, AND TEACHING THEM TO OBEY EVERYTHING I HAVE COMMANDED YOU. AND SURELY I AM WITH YOU ALWAYS, TO THE VERY END OF THE AGE. — MATTHEW 28:18-20

Based on this passage, where does Jesus have authority?

What is Jesus telling us to do? Underline every command Jesus gives in the above passage.

Whom is He telling us to disciple?

After we have made disciples, what then is our responsibility?

Finally, at the end of this passage, what does Jesus remind us? Underline it in purple.

Jesus has all authority in Heaven and on earth. Since He now lives implanted within us through the Holy Spirit, we share His authority and we are therefore equipped and empowered to go and make disciples of the nations. Through Him, we have all we need to do this task of making disciples of all the nations—to go out into the harvest fields of all the earth!

Notice that the command to make disciples requires more than just bringing them to salvation; it also requires us to teach them and train them in knowing God's Word and walking in His ways. This is called *discipleship*. It too is a labor of the harvest.

"Surely, I am with you always." Jesus is reminding us that we do not go out into the vast harvest fields alone or independently. It would be impossible to accomplish anything for Him in our own strength. Remember our lessons on abiding and fruit bearing. We are a branch clinging to Christ, our Vine, and we receive everything from Him. He is the source of all we are and all we do. He does not merely send us out into the harvest fields; He accompanies us!

Now let's look at Romans 10:14-15:

> HOW, THEN, CAN THEY CALL ON THE ONE THEY HAVE NOT BELIEVED IN? AND HOW CAN THEY BELIEVE IN THE ONE OF WHOM THEY HAVE NOT HEARD? AND HOW CAN THEY HEAR WITHOUT SOMEONE PREACHING TO THEM? AND HOW CAN THEY PREACH UNLESS THEY ARE SENT? AS IT IS WRITTEN, "HOW BEAUTIFUL ARE THE FEET OF THOSE WHO BRING GOOD NEWS!"—ROMANS 10:14-15

What is this passage saying to you? What is the problem and what is the solution?

Do you want to have beautiful feet? What makes your feet beautiful to the Lord of the Harvest?

Jesus no longer walks the earth in His physical body, but He still has a physical body. It is His Church, it's us—we who have His life living within our hearts. We are now His hands, His feet, and His mouth. "How shall they hear without a preacher?" We are all called to preach—to speak forth and proclaim the glad tidings of good news (Romans 10:15).

We are carrying forth the ageless message that the angels first brought to mankind on the hillside outside of Bethlehem thousands of years ago. Luke 2:10 says, "Do not be afraid, for behold, I bring you good tidings of great joy which will be to all people" (New King James Version). Then the angel goes on to tell them of Christ, the One who will save them. We have the same message of the angels! We are now carrying on the proclamation that the angels began. We are now the heralds bringing the good news of the gospel—the glad tidings of good things! This message is Jesus! There is no better news for mankind.

Vi's Gardening Tip:

How will the nations know about Jesus unless we tell them? It is an awesome calling to go out into the harvest fields and speak the good news of Jesus! What is your answer to this great invitation extended to you by the Lord of the Harvest? Will you answer like Isaiah did in Isaiah 6:8: "Here am I; Send me!"? You can make a difference no matter where you are—one soul at a time. God has a special plan for you in His great harvest. Will you put your hand to the plow?

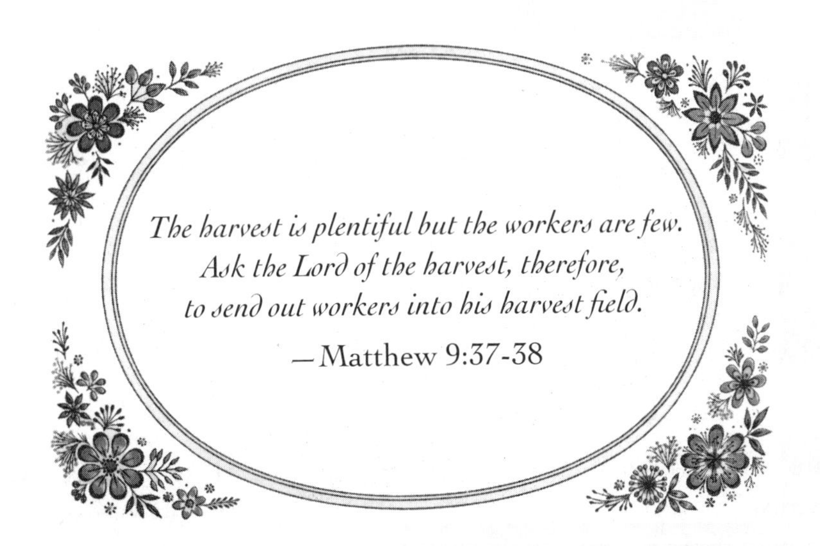

The harvest is plentiful but the workers are few.
Ask the Lord of the harvest, therefore,
to send out workers into his harvest field.
—Matthew 9:37-38

Lesson Twenty-Seven

THE HARVEST FIELDS

How beautiful is a field of ripened grain—the amber glow of a wheat field swaying like gold in the breeze. Can you imagine the delight it brings to the farmer and his anticipation of a bountiful harvest? It is the fruit of his labor—the promise of abundance!

> DO YOU NOT SAY, "FOUR MONTHS MORE AND THEN THE HARVEST"? I TELL YOU, OPEN YOUR EYES AND LOOK AT THE FIELDS! THEY ARE RIPE FOR HARVEST. EVEN NOW THE REAPER DRAWS HIS WAGES, EVEN NOW HE HARVESTS THE CROP FOR ETERNAL LIFE, SO THAT THE SOWER AND THE REAPER MAY BE GLAD TOGETHER. —JOHN 4:35-36

Jesus told His disciples that souls were ripe and ready to receive the good news of the gospel. "Lift up your eyes!" as Jesus said. What do *you* see? Can you see the harvest field in front of you? There is a "harvest field" wherever your "beautiful feet" carry you. It is God's harvest field—where you will find people whose hearts are hungry to hear and understand the good news of Jesus. Some people are called to harvest in fields abroad. These we call *missionaries*. Others harvest in fields that lie in their own backyards. Whether at home or abroad, no matter where your harvest field, you are called to the exciting and joyous work of a missionary.

As a spiritual harvester, you have an assignment that only you can do. You have been strategically planted in a specific harvest field by the Lord of the Harvest. You have special friends and relationships with people that no one else has. You have seeds to plant in your harvest field that no one else can plant. How will the people in your harvest field know the depths of Christ's love without someone to show them? Lift up your eyes and look with fresh vision at your harvest field. See the amazing potential for fruitfulness right where you are!

Reflection:

Take some time to reflect on your own harvest fields. Where are they?

List the people in your harvest fields who you think could be ripe to receive the good news of Jesus. Next to their names, list some ways you might be able to plant seeds in their hearts:

Would you like to harvest in a foreign land someday? If so, where? If not, where else could you see yourself harvesting in the future?

Trust the Lord of the Harvest to lead you into your appointed harvest fields. Get excited! You were chosen to be the herald of good news in your own harvest field! When your season of harvesting in one field is finished, He will lead you to another. Right now your harvest field may be your school, swim class, or neighborhood. Of course, your family will always be a harvest field. In the future, your harvest field may change. You may be planted on a college campus, working in an office, or living in a subdivision. Be content and faithful in each and every harvest field. In other words, "Bloom where you are planted." Look with fresh eyes at your life and recognize the potential for harvest all around you.

You can trust the Lord of the Harvest. Let the Holy Spirit lead you as you step into your harvest fields. You won't be able to reach everyone. Remember our lessons on the different types of soil. *The Holy Spirit will show you which people in your harvest field have soft soil that is ready to receive the seeds of the gospel. For others, the soil will first need to be softened by planting seeds of kindness and service.*

Our number one goal in the work of the harvest is to sow the gospel, which is the good news of Jesus Christ. We sow the gospel in many ways. Let's look at two of the most powerful seeds you can sow.

First, we sow the Word of God. We must understand how powerful God's Word really is. Hebrews 4:12 says that God's Word is "living and active." It has power to create, just as God spoke creation into existence through His Word. Isaiah 55:11 says that God's Word will accomplish what God intended it to accomplish. God's Word is moving toward a purpose. It is living and therefore growing and bearing fruit all over the world.

Read the following Scriptures. Using your colored pencils, underline any words or phrases that describe the "living" nature of God's Word. We'll get you started:

ALL OVER THE WORLD THIS GOSPEL IS BEARING FRUIT AND GROWING, JUST AS IT HAS BEEN DOING AMONG YOU SINCE THE DAY YOU HEARD IT AND UNDERSTOOD GOD'S GRACE IN ALL ITS TRUTH. —COLOSSIANS 1:6

BUT THE WORD OF GOD CONTINUED TO INCREASE AND SPREAD. —ACTS 12:24

IN THIS WAY THE WORD OF THE LORD SPREAD WIDELY AND GREW IN POWER. —ACTS 19:20

Have faith and be confident when you share God's Word. You are sowing very powerful seeds that will grow and increase in power. Remember, God causes His Word to grow in the hearts of men. If the soil is good, the Word will grow. *We are responsible for sowing the seed of God's Word into hearts. We are not responsible for its growth and fruitfulness.* That is God's responsibility, and we will become weary and frustrated if we take on God's responsibility.

I PLANTED THE SEED, APOLLOS WATERED IT, BUT GOD MADE IT GROW. SO NEITHER HE WHO PLANTS NOR HE WHO WATERS IS ANYTHING, BUT ONLY GOD, WHO MAKES THINGS GROW. —1 CORINTHIANS 3:6-7

Trust God for each seed that you sow. Water them with lots of prayer and then be patient and full of faith. Some gospel seeds may lie dormant in a heart for quite some time until the soil of the heart is soft enough to allow for growth.

Secondly, we sow our very lives. We must let the life of Christ live through us powerfully and authentically. One way we do this is through the way we conduct ourselves and treat others. This is probably as important as, if not more important than, sowing God's Word.

Let's look at what God's Word teaches us. Draw a flower around the phrase "good deeds":

You are the light of the world. A city on a hill cannot be hidden. . . . In the same way, let your light shine before men, that they may see your good deeds and praise your Father in heaven. —Matthew 5:14, 16

You must shine the light of Christ on your harvest field through your behavior, through acts of kindness, love, help, and mercy. You are a living example of Christ. Your actions will speak louder than words. Those in your harvest field will read your life before they will read the Bible. Second Corinthians 3:2 says, "You yourselves are our letter, written on our hearts, known and read by everybody." Let your light shine so radiantly that they see the face of Christ when they look at you.

Vi's Gardening Tip:

The thought of sharing your faith may be intimidating. But do not be afraid of your mission field. It may look awfully dark at times, and you may feel alone and insignificant, or even insecure. But do not be dismayed, for God is with you! Remember the words of Jesus: "Surely, I am with you always!"

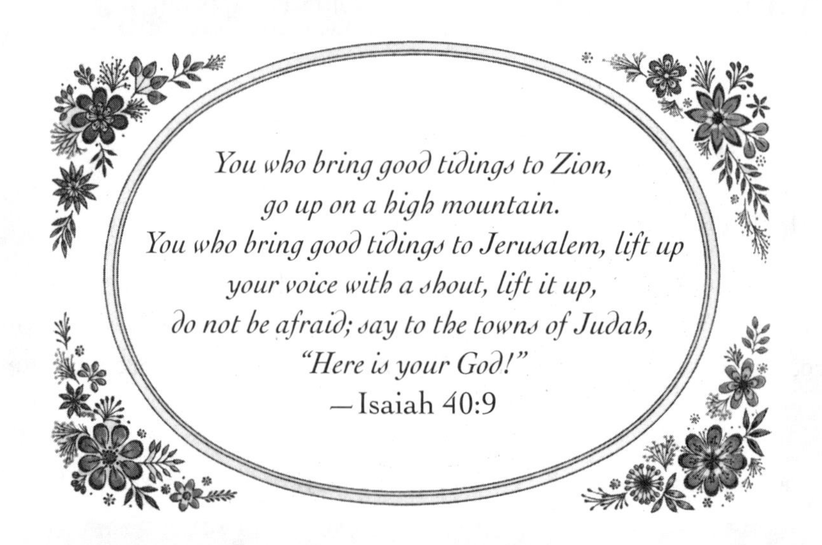

You who bring good tidings to Zion,
go up on a high mountain.
You who bring good tidings to Jerusalem, lift up
your voice with a shout, lift it up,
do not be afraid; say to the towns of Judah,
"Here is your God!"
—Isaiah 40:9

Lesson Twenty-Eight

Your Seed Bag

As we have already learned in our garden lessons, seeds in the natural realm come in various shapes and sizes. So it is in the spiritual realm. There are a variety of seeds we can sow into our harvest fields. Each seed sown has the capacity in it to produce its own unique fruit. As a spiritual harvester, the Lord of the Harvest has given you your very own special bag of seeds that no one else has. Your seeds are given to you for your provision, but there is a much greater purpose for these seeds. They have been given to you to scatter onto your harvest fields for the purpose of producing a great harvest in the lives of others.

What is in your seed bag? The many varieties of seeds you may find will include the following: your time, your money, your gifts and talents, the Word of God, prayer, kind deeds, and acts of help and mercy, just to name a few.

Let's learn some important principles about seed-sowing from the following Scripture:

> Remember this: Whoever sows sparingly will also reap sparingly, and whoever sows generously will also reap generously. Each man should give what he has decided in his heart to give, not reluctantly or under compulsion, for God loves a cheerful giver. And God is able to make all grace abound to you, so that in all

THINGS AT ALL TIMES, HAVING ALL THAT YOU NEED, YOU WILL ABOUND IN EVERY GOOD WORK. AS IT IS WRITTEN: "HE HAS SCATTERED ABROAD HIS GIFTS TO THE POOR; HIS RIGHTEOUSNESS ENDURES FOREVER." NOW HE WHO SUPPLIES SEED TO THE SOWER AND BREAD FOR FOOD WILL ALSO SUPPLY AND INCREASE YOUR STORE OF SEED AND WILL ENLARGE THE HARVEST OF YOUR RIGHTEOUSNESS. —2 CORINTHIANS 9:6-10

This passage was intended to speak about the seed of money, but the principles of giving remain the same regardless of what seed you are sowing. What is a very important principle of sowing and harvesting that we should note? If you sow sparingly, you will reap ______________. If you sow generously, you will also reap _________________.

The amount of harvest reaped is directly related to the amount of seeds sown. A few seeds will produce a few plants, but two packs of seeds will bring forth several rows of plants!

Who supplies us with our seeds?

God not only supplies our seed, but what else does He do with the bag of seeds that He has given us?

Go back to 2 Corinthians 9:6-10. Draw an apple around the words "good work" in this passage (remember, we talked about bearing fruit as being "good works"). Next, circle the word "all" each time it appears.

What is the promise we are given in our seed-sowing and our fruitfulness? Record your answer below:

The Lord of the Harvest will supply you with all the seed you need to accomplish every good work that He has planned for you. The more you sow the seeds He gives you, the more seed

He will provide. Your seed bag will be ever overflowing. But the secret is in the scattering. If you are faithful to scatter your seeds when He leads you, He will be faithful to make sure that you will always have an abundance of seed in your bag.

Once again, go back to 2 Corinthians 9:6-10. This time, underline the two places where you see the word "righteousness." What will the Lord do for the person who faithfully and sacrificially scatters her seed (or her gifts) in His harvest field to help others?

The Lord of the Harvest will cause an abundant, overflowing, and lasting harvest of righteousness to spring forth in the sower's life. Proverbs 11:24 says, "One man gives freely, yet gains even more; another withholds unduly, but comes to poverty."

All that we are and all that we have really belong to the Lord. James 1:17 reminds us that "every good and perfect gift is from above." We must remember that what we have been given is temporarily loaned to us to use during this short stay on earth. We are to be responsible stewards with this bag of seeds. Romans 11:36 says, "For from him and through him and to him are all things. To him be the glory forever! Amen."

Reflection:

Now it's time to take inventory of the various seeds you have in your seed bag. What seeds have you been given that you can sow into your harvest field? Refer back to the beginning of this lesson for examples.

How can you sow these seeds? Write your thoughts below:

You might be looking at a tiny seed in your bag, shaking your head, and wondering how this little insignificant seed can make a difference. For example, maybe you can sing well, but you don't think you're good enough to join the youth choir. You are looking at how small or ugly your seed appears, instead of looking at the Lord of the Harvest. Never be deceived by the size or appearance of the seed! Trust the Lord of the Harvest. He is the one who makes all things grow. He has a green thumb! He not only makes the seed grow, but He also increases and multiplies it. Trust Him with your seed. Be bold! Join that choir and sow the talent that God has given you. He will use your voice to be a blessing to others. Sow in faith.

Listen to what Jesus said about a small seed:

> WHAT SHALL WE SAY THE KINGDOM OF GOD IS LIKE, OR WHAT PARABLE SHALL WE USE TO DESCRIBE IT? IT IS LIKE A MUSTARD SEED, WHICH IS THE SMALLEST SEED YOU PLANT IN THE GROUND. YET WHEN PLANTED, IT GROWS AND BECOMES THE LARGEST OF ALL GARDEN PLANTS, WITH SUCH BIG BRANCHES THAT THE BIRDS OF THE AIR CAN PERCH IN ITS SHADE.
> —MARK 4:30-32

When planted, this mustard seed grew and became a large plant. How was this plant useful?

The plant became shade, shelter, and a resting place for the birds. You, too, can trust that the Lord of the Harvest will do the same with your life and the seeds you plant. You can offer comfort, support, and strength to those who pass your way.

The mustard seed referred to in this parable was believed to be the common black mustard. Its seeds were cultivated for their oil and other cooking uses. The seed of this plant was close to the size of a pinhead and was well known to the people in the Galilee area. This explains why Jesus chose it as an illustration. The black mustard is really an herb and it may grow 10-12 feet high with a stem the size of a man's arm. These plants could easily provide a resting place for smaller variety of birds.

DAISY
SEEDS OF INTEREST
MORE ON THE MUSTARD SEED

Vi's Gardening Tip:

Give freely and unashamedly any seed in your seed bag to the Lord of the Harvest. Put that tiny, little seed into His big, capable hand and watch Him work a miracle. Remember the boy who brought Jesus his lunch of five small barley loaves and two small fish? Jesus took that small "seed" offering, multiplied it, and fed 5,000 people! Give your seed, no matter how seemingly small and insignificant, to the Lord of the Harvest and trust Him to do with it what only He can do—multiply it out and work a miracle!

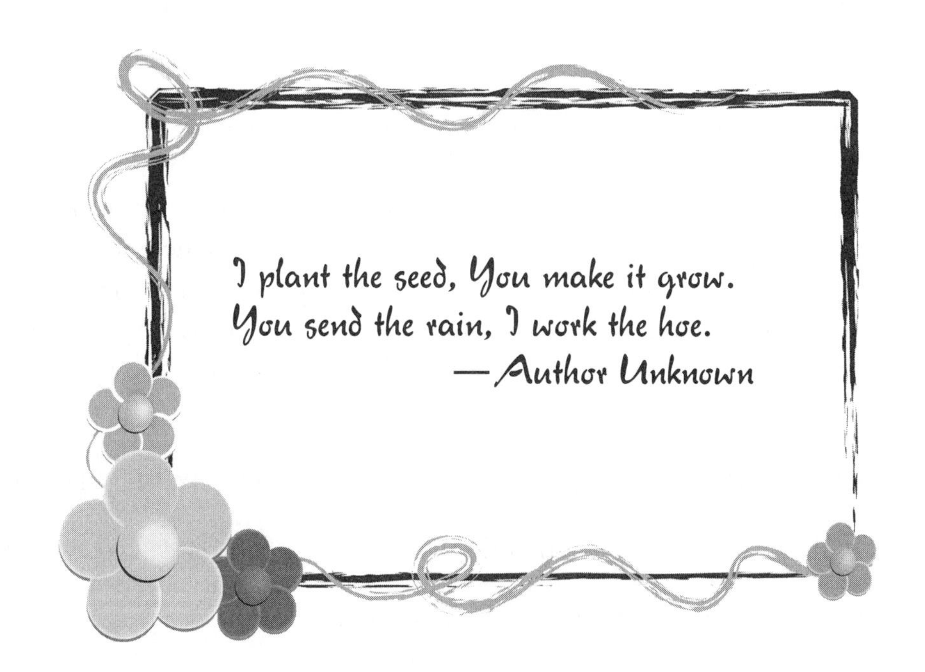

I plant the seed, You make it grow.
You send the rain, I work the hoe.
—Author Unknown

Lesson Twenty-Nine

The Faithful and Focused Harvester

Genesis 8:22 says, "As long as the earth endures, seedtime and harvest, cold and heat, summer and winter, day and night will never cease." Just as we have seasons in our natural world, so we have seasons in our spiritual lives, too. Ecclesiastes 3:2 tells us there is a time to sow (plant) and a time to reap (to pluck). The season of sowing will eventually give way to a season of reaping. Anything that will reap a great reward has a price tag. It will cost you hard work, perseverance, and commitment—sometimes to the point of sacrifice. Still, we must never lose sight of the joy of reaping while we are sweating in our harvest fields. Examine the following verse:

> THOSE WHO SOW IN TEARS WILL REAP WITH SONGS OF JOY. HE WHO GOES OUT WEEPING, CARRYING SEED TO SOW, WILL RETURN WITH SONGS OF JOY, CARRYING SHEAVES WITH HIM. —PSALM 126:5-6

After the wheat stalks were cut down (reaped), they were tied in bundles called *sheaves*. The sheaves were then taken to be threshed. (Refer to Section 2 in the Appendix for more information about this process.) The sheaves in this verse represent the fruitfulness, the harvest of righteousness, and the abundant blessing that finally came from the tearful sowing.

What do you think it means to sow in tears?

REFLECTION:

Is there a situation in your life now where you feel you are sowing in tears? Are you having trouble standing for the Lord at school or at home? Have you been praying a long time for someone to accept Christ and it hasn't happened yet? Briefly explain below:

Sowing seeds in your harvest field will not always be an easy task. It often requires great measures of faithfulness in areas like denying yourself, long-suffering, and patience—which at times will be difficult. Your character will be tested. Sometimes you may literally water the seeds with your tears. But you must never lose sight of the joy of the harvest and the reaping that is sure to come from your diligence.

We mentioned earlier in our garden study that our job is to plant the seeds—God's job is to bring the growth. We must trust Him with the timing. He has a "proper" season for the seeds to bear fruit and the harvest to begin. His "proper" season will happen in His perfect timing.

Underline the action phrases that the following Scriptures encourage you to do:

> LET US NOT BECOME WEARY IN DOING GOOD, FOR AT THE PROPER TIME WE WILL REAP A HARVEST IF WE DO NOT GIVE UP. —GALATIANS 6:9

> THEREFORE, MY DEAR BROTHERS, STAND FIRM. LET NOTHING MOVE YOU. ALWAYS GIVE YOURSELVES FULLY TO THE WORK OF THE LORD, BECAUSE YOU KNOW THAT YOUR LABOR IN THE LORD IS NOT IN VAIN. —1 CORINTHIANS 15:58

Growing and maturing in Christ often requires us to remain faithful in doing what is right, even when we don't see immediate results. We are called to live by faith, not by sight (2 Corinthians 5:7), and that includes our work in the harvest fields. By faith we sow, knowing we will reap in God's perfect time.

Below, write an example (in your life or another's) when a harvest finally came after many years of faithfully sowing.

Sometimes we may not see the fruition of our harvest until we see things fully in Heaven. But, oh what rejoicing then! What greater reward than to see someday the sheaves of souls that you had a hand in harvesting, and to hear your precious Lord say, "Well done, good and faithful servant. You have been faithful over a little; I will set you over much. Enter into the joy of your master" (Matthew 25:23, English Standard Version). You will be singing the song of the harvest with joy unimaginable! Never grow weary in sowing good and righteous seeds into your harvest fields. Stand firm in believing that your harvest will come. Persevere and remain faithful to the very end for the sure-to-come harvest!

Joy

In Luke 9:62, Jesus taught another farming parable to illustrate the importance of staying focused while working the harvest field: "No one who puts his hand to the plow and looks back is fit for service in the kingdom of God." To understand the meaning of this verse, it is helpful to know a bit about plowing. To ensure nice, straight furrows (long, narrow, shallow trenches for planting) when plowing, a farmer must keep his eyes fixed on an object in the distant horizon, which acts as his aiming point. If he is constantly looking back where he has plowed, he will lose his focus and his furrows will end up like squiggly lines. (For more information about plowing, refer to Section 2 in the Appendix.)

Jesus used this parable to illustrate the importance of not losing sight of the incredible purpose and mission we have been given to harvest souls for God's Kingdom. "Looking back" in our Christian lives could mean getting distracted by things of the world, becoming half-hearted, wavering in our faithfulness, or becoming double-minded (James 1:8). It can even mean pridefully looking back on our accomplishments and successes. We can lose our edge for effective plowing if we constantly lose our focus and "look back."

What things distract you from keeping your eyes focused on the call to be a harvester? Write your thoughts below:

When doing the work of harvesting, we do not want to lose our bearings. If we are always distracted, our eyes will lose the precious landmark ahead—Christ and His Kingdom. This will prevent us from reaching our greatest fruitfulness for Jesus. That's what Jesus meant by not being "fit" for the Kingdom of God. To be *fit* means to be useful for the purpose—at maximum potential and effectiveness.

We all "look back" every now and then. It's easy to lose sight of what is really important in our lives. Jesus isn't saying that when this happens you aren't worthy to be His disciple. He's just saying that half-hearted commitment will produce poor results for you and His Kingdom. You will waste a lot of time wandering around your harvest field, going in circles, and wasting daylight when you could be participating in the joyful and exciting work of the harvest, making disciples of Christ—a worthwhile endeavor with everlasting and eternal results!

Vi's Gardening Tip:

Remember, our labor in the harvest is a partnership with God. We work as the Spirit of Christ within directs and empowers us. Jesus invites us to yoke up with Him in this harvest labor. He says that His yoke is easy and His burden is light and we will find rest for our souls. There is still a job to do; we must still plow and there will always be a weight to pull in this life, but when we are yoked up with Jesus, He takes the weight of our burdens and the plowing is restful, light, and even joyful.

Come to me, all you who are weary and burdened, and I will give you rest. Take my yoke upon you and learn from me, for I am gentle and humble in heart, and you will find rest for your souls. For my yoke is easy and my burden is light.

—Matthew 11:28-30

Lesson Thirty

The Final Harvest

What a wonderful journey we have shared together—the personal journey of growing toward God in the garden of our hearts and then pouring out the abundance of our growth to touch others in God's harvest fields. You are special and chosen, called by the Lord of the Harvest to do something unique in His Kingdom. Our prayer is that this study has helped to equip you for your calling. Most of all, we pray that you will truly know the joy of serving the Lord and of abiding with Him in the secret garden of your heart.

Our study started out like a single seed that has been "growing and growing." Now we have reached the end. But this final lesson is really about a new beginning. For now we turn our attention to God's final harvest, which is the time in history when God will gather together all of His children (those who have the Seed of God planted and growing in their hearts) from the entire earth, both living and dead. He will harvest those who are righteous and they will live with Him forever. God's final harvest is our final destination—it is the blessed destiny and promise of every believer!

We've come so far in our garden study together. Let's do a quick re-cap. We learned about planting seeds, tending and caring for those seeds, and the harvesting that happens in our hearts as a result. Jesus, the Seed of God, is planted in our hearts. He grows inside of us and bears fruit that the Master Gardener then harvests and uses for His glory. This fruit comes in the form of qualities, character, and attributes that are Christlike and produce good works. When our gardens mature and begin to become fruitful, we then venture out into the harvest fields of the world to partner with the Lord of the Harvest in the harvesting of souls. Remember, to *harvest* means to gather in. This work in the harvest fields will continue until the time is ripe and the harvest fields of the earth are ready for the final, great, and awesome harvest of God.

Jesus again used an agricultural analogy to tell us about this great harvest to come. (To learn more background information on this parable, refer to "Weeds and Wheat" in Section 2 of the Appendix.) He then explained the analogy to His disciples to make sure they understood.

Let's look at His teaching together. Take your time to read through the following passage. Using your colored pencils, circle the word "weed" in brown and circle the word "wheat" in yellow. Draw pictures over any other words that are important to you:

> JESUS TOLD THEM ANOTHER PARABLE: "THE KINGDOM OF HEAVEN IS LIKE A MAN WHO SOWED GOOD SEED IN HIS FIELD. BUT WHILE EVERYONE WAS SLEEPING, HIS ENEMY CAME AND SOWED WEEDS AMONG THE WHEAT, AND WENT AWAY. WHEN THE WHEAT SPROUTED AND FORMED HEADS, THEN THE WEEDS ALSO APPEARED. THE OWNER'S SERVANTS CAME TO HIM AND SAID, 'SIR, DIDN'T YOU SOW GOOD SEED IN YOUR FIELD? WHERE THEN DID THE WEEDS COME FROM?' 'AN ENEMY DID THIS,' HE REPLIED. THE SERVANTS ASKED HIM, 'DO YOU WANT US TO GO AND PULL THEM UP?' 'NO,' HE ANSWERED, 'BECAUSE WHILE YOU ARE PULLING THE WEEDS, YOU MAY ROOT UP THE WHEAT WITH THEM. LET BOTH GROW TOGETHER UNTIL THE HARVEST. AT THAT TIME I WILL TELL THE HARVESTERS: FIRST COLLECT THE WEEDS AND TIE THEM IN BUNDLES TO BE BURNED; THEN GATHER THE WHEAT AND BRING IT INTO MY BARN.'" THEN HE LEFT THE CROWD AND WENT INTO THE HOUSE. HIS DISCIPLES CAME TO HIM AND SAID, "EXPLAIN TO US THE PARABLE OF THE WEEDS IN THE FIELD." HE ANSWERED, "THE

ONE WHO SOWED THE GOOD SEED IS THE SON OF MAN. THE FIELD IS THE WORLD, AND THE GOOD SEED STANDS FOR THE SONS OF THE KINGDOM. THE WEEDS ARE THE SONS OF THE EVIL ONE, AND THE ENEMY WHO SOWS THEM IS THE DEVIL. THE HARVEST IS THE END OF THE AGE, AND THE HARVESTERS ARE ANGELS. AS THE WEEDS ARE PULLED UP AND BURNED IN THE FIRE, SO IT WILL BE AT THE END OF THE AGE. THE SON OF MAN WILL SEND OUT HIS ANGELS, AND THEY WILL WEED OUT OF HIS KINGDOM EVERYTHING THAT CAUSES SIN AND ALL WHO DO EVIL. THEY WILL THROW THEM INTO THE FIERY FURNACE, WHERE THERE WILL BE WEEPING AND GNASHING OF TEETH. THEN THE RIGHTEOUS WILL SHINE LIKE THE SUN IN THE KINGDOM OF THEIR FATHER. HE WHO HAS EARS, LET HIM HEAR."

—MATTHEW 13:24-30, 36-43

Matthew 24:36 tells us that only the Lord of the Harvest knows when it's time for Him to reap from His great harvest field, the earth. But we do know that the day will come like a thief in the night and will catch many unprepared. Jesus said at the end of the parable above, "He who has ears, let him hear." In other words, don't just hear, but let it affect how you live your life. Do not be as those who are caught unaware and unprepared! Live each day with an eye to the sky, expecting your Lord to return for you that day!

Read the passage below and underline how we ought to be living.

BUT THE DAY OF THE LORD WILL COME LIKE A THIEF. THE HEAVENS WILL DISAPPEAR WITH A ROAR; THE ELEMENTS WILL BE DESTROYED BY FIRE, AND THE EARTH AND EVERYTHING IN IT WILL BE LAID BARE. SINCE EVERYTHING WILL BE DESTROYED IN THIS WAY, WHAT KIND OF PEOPLE OUGHT YOU TO BE? YOU OUGHT TO LIVE HOLY AND GODLY LIVES AS YOU LOOK FORWARD

TO THE DAY OF GOD AND SPEED ITS COMING. THAT DAY WILL BRING ABOUT THE DESTRUCTION OF THE HEAVENS BY FIRE, AND THE ELEMENTS WILL MELT IN THE HEAT. BUT IN KEEPING WITH HIS PROMISE WE ARE LOOKING FORWARD TO A NEW HEAVEN AND A NEW EARTH, THE HOME OF RIGHTEOUSNESS. SO THEN, DEAR FRIENDS, SINCE YOU ARE LOOKING FORWARD TO THIS, MAKE EVERY EFFORT TO BE FOUND SPOTLESS, BLAMELESS AND AT PEACE WITH HIM. —2 PETER 3:10-14

REFLECTION:

How would you live today if you knew that Christ was coming for you tomorrow? Think about it for a moment. What would you change? With whom would you reconcile? Jot down some things you would do or the people you would talk to. Consider writing some letters to express your gratitude or an apology to someone.

What is the Lord saying to you? Write your thoughts below:

The Lord's return will be sudden, but it will also be a glorious event. Look with joy and expectancy at His coming. We do not need to fear His return. Always remember that the grace of God is here for us. He knows that we are not perfect and He is compassionate toward our weaknesses. We can "watch and pray" and seek God's direction for our lives each and every day. Believe that He will reveal any "unfinished business" in your life—and then honor Him by responding to His promptings.

When that glorious hour does come, Jesus will appear in the clouds and the final, great harvest will begin!

> I LOOKED, AND THERE BEFORE ME WAS A WHITE CLOUD, AND SEATED ON THE CLOUD WAS ONE "LIKE A SON OF MAN" WITH A CROWN OF GOLD ON HIS HEAD AND A SHARP SICKLE IN HIS HAND. THEN ANOTHER ANGEL CAME OUT OF THE TEMPLE AND CALLED IN A LOUD VOICE TO HIM WHO WAS SITTING ON THE CLOUD, "TAKE YOUR SICKLE AND REAP, BECAUSE THE TIME TO REAP HAS COME, FOR THE HARVEST OF THE EARTH IS RIPE." SO HE WHO WAS SEATED ON THE CLOUD SWUNG HIS SICKLE OVER THE EARTH, AND THE EARTH WAS HARVESTED. —REVELATION 14:14-16 (REFER TO SECTION 2 IN THE APPENDIX FOR MORE INFORMATION ABOUT HARVESTING AND REAPING.)

> AND HE WILL SEND HIS ANGELS WITH A LOUD TRUMPET CALL, AND THEY WILL GATHER HIS ELECT FROM THE FOUR WINDS, FROM ONE END OF THE HEAVENS TO THE OTHER. —MATTHEW 24:31

These heavenly harvesters will first weed out those who are evil and then tie them in bundles and cast onto a pile to be burned. Then those who have loved righteousness will be gathered together in God's Kingdom where they will shine forever like the sun. This will be the culmination of the joy of the Lord of the Harvest. The song of the harvest will resound in its greatest refrain. Listen to it!

> THEN I HEARD EVERY CREATURE IN HEAVEN AND ON EARTH AND UNDER THE EARTH AND ON THE SEA, AND ALL THAT IS IN THEM, SINGING: "TO HIM WHO SITS ON THE THRONE AND TO THE LAMB BE PRAISE AND HONOR AND GLORY AND POWER, FOR EVER AND EVER!" —REVELATION 5:13

There will be another kind of harvesting on this day. It will be an individual reaping for everyone according to the seeds they have sown—how they have lived their lives. All those good seeds that each person has sown will come to full maturity; everyone's fruit will be revealed and each will reap and be rewarded for his or her good works.

For the Son of Man is going to come in his Father's glory with his angels, and then he will reward each person according to what he has done. —Matthew 16:27

I have fought the good fight, I have finished the race, I have kept the faith. Now there is in store for me the crown of righteousness, which the Lord, the righteous Judge, will award to me on that day—and not only to me, but also to all who have longed for his appearing. —2 Timothy 4:7-8

What do you think the rewards might be? Paul mentioned a crown of righteousness. Imagine the most spectacular rewards you would like to receive and write them below.

There are no words to describe the joy and delight awaiting those who will be harvested into God's Kingdom, a place where the Lord will wipe every tear from our eyes, and where there will be no more death or mourning or crying or pain. Mark any words or phrases that stand out to you in the following verses.

They are before the throne of God and serve him day and night in his temple; and he who sits on the throne will spread his tent over them. Never again will they hunger; never again will they thirst. The sun will not beat upon them, nor any scorching heat. For the Lamb at the center of the throne will be their shepherd; he will lead them to springs of living water. And God will wipe away every tear from their eyes. —Revelation 7:15-17

Do you remember in Lesson 1 when we stood at the gate of the Garden of Eden and peered inside? The tree of life was standing in the middle of the garden and it provided health, happiness, and life. Through our journey together we've learned that Christ is now our Tree of Life who stands in the middle of our gardens and brings life and healing for all the nations of the world!

In our final moments together, let's take one last peek through another gate—a gate that looks upon a magnificent, celestial city—and see what eternal delights abide within. As you peer inside, think about all the lessons you've learned in the garden of your heart. Imagine yourself opening this ancient gate and stepping inside:

> Then the angel showed me the river of the water of life, as clear as crystal, flowing from the throne of God and of the Lamb down the middle of the great street of the city. On each side of the river stood the tree of life, bearing twelve crops of fruit, yielding its fruit every month. And the leaves of the tree are for the healing of the nations. No longer will there be any curse. The throne of God and of the Lamb will be in the city, and his servants will serve him. They will see his face, and his name will be on their foreheads. There will be no more night. They will not need the light of a lamp or the light of the sun, for the Lord God will give them light. And they will reign for ever and ever. The angel said to me, These words are trustworthy and true. The Lord, the God of the spirits of the prophets, sent his angel to show his servants the things that must soon take place.—Revelation 22:1-6

Look! There's the crystal river! Water is flowing in abundance! There's the tree of life—it stands in the middle of the city, full of healing fruit! The curse is gone! There is no more darkness! God's presence is the source of light! Everything is thriving and growing in this heavenly place!

In this great city, our fellowship and joy with the Lord will far exceed the communion Adam and Eve experienced in the Garden of Eden, and it will even exceed the intimacy we've enjoyed with Him in the garden of our hearts. For when we walk through the gates of this city, we shall see the Master Gardener face-to-face in all His splendor! We will know Him fully and dwell in His kingdom. We will flourish in His courts forever and ever! Amen and Amen.

> BLESSED ARE THOSE WHO WASH THEIR ROBES, THAT THEY MAY HAVE THE RIGHT TO THE TREE OF LIFE AND MAY GO THROUGH THE GATES INTO THE CITY. —REVELATION 22:14

Vi's Gardening Tip:

Receive and rejoice in all that is yours as a child of God. Embrace your Master Gardener with abandon and let Him lead you on an amazing journey of faith. There is no greater joy—there is no greater purpose in this life—than growing toward God in the garden of your heart. Trust Him. Take His hand. Receive His love. And always, dear friend, always lift your face to the Son!

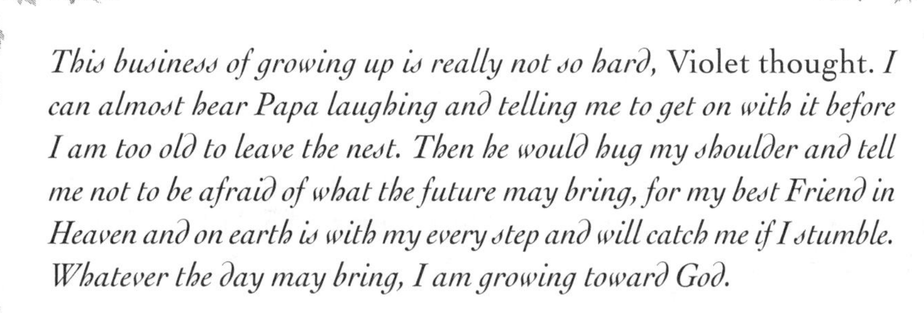

This business of growing up is really not so hard, Violet thought. *I can almost hear Papa laughing and telling me to get on with it before I am too old to leave the nest. Then he would hug my shoulder and tell me not to be afraid of what the future may bring, for my best Friend in Heaven and on earth is with my every step and will catch me if I stumble. Whatever the day may bring, I am growing toward God.*

—*Violet's Hidden Doubts*

APPENDIX

Section 1

OLD TESTAMENT LAND LAWS

- The soil was to lie fallow (given a rest) every seventh year and every 50th year to keep the land fertile and to prevent it from losing valuable nutrients from overuse. Whatever the land produces on its own may be eaten. (Leviticus 25:3-7, 11-12)
- It was forbidden to sow the land with 2 different kinds of seeds. (Leviticus 19:19)
- The carcass (body of a dead animal) and water together cannot touch the seeds to be planted. They are considered "unclean." (Leviticus 11:38)
- The corners of the fields and other gleanings were to be left for the poor to gather. This law is seen in action in the book of Ruth, a wonderful story and a must-read. In it, we find Ruth, a Moabite widow, gleaning among the poor in the fields. Boaz, the kind owner of the field, orders his workers to leave extra stalks lying behind for Ruth to glean. (Ruth 2:15-17)
- The firstfruits of all crops belonged to Jehovah and were brought to the temple. (Exodus 34:26)
- "When you enter the land and plant any kind of fruit tree, regard its fruit as forbidden. For three years you are to consider it forbidden; it must not be eaten. In the fourth year all its fruit will be holy, an offering of praise to the Lord. But in the fifth year you may eat its fruit. In this way your harvest will be increased. I am the LORD your God." (Leviticus 19:23-25)
- "A tithe of everything from the land, whether grain from the soil or fruit from the trees, belongs to the LORD; it is holy to the LORD." (Leviticus 27:30)
- You could pass by a neighbor's field and eat all the grapes or grain you wanted, as long as you didn't carry any away (Deuteronomy 23:24-25). See an example of this in Matthew 12:1.

Section 2

Agriculture in Bible Times

Climate and Crops of the Holy Land

After herding animals, tilling the ground was the next main occupation in Biblical times. Adam and Eve were given the assignment to cultivate and tend the Garden of Eden. This type of occupation continued on in some form through Abraham, Isaac, and Jacob, but it wasn't until the Israelites were taken captive in Egypt for 400 years that they really learned about agriculture. The Egyptians excelled in agriculture and the Israelites learned well. God uses all things for good. After God delivered Israel from Egypt, He led them to the promised land of Canaan. There the soil was fertile and the conditions were ideal for crops to grow. Consequently agriculture became the foundation of Israel's economy and culture.

In order to gain more insight into the agriculture of Israel, where the Israelites lived, we must have an understanding about this land's climate. Israel is a small geographical area and yet has quite a variety of geographical terrains, which allow for a wide range of temperatures and amounts of rain. Some mountains in Israel, such as Mount Hermon, reach up to 9,000 feet above sea level, while other areas like the Dead Sea reach to the depths of 1,292 feet below sea level. It is common to find snow on the mountains and tropical fruit ripening on the plains, all at the same time.

There are basically two major seasons in Israel – the hot, dry summer, which extends uninterrupted from mid-June to mid-September, and the rainy season, which occurs intermittently for the rest of the year. Cold weather is limited to a three-month period starting in mid-December. Because the rainy seasons were unpredictable in Biblical times, famines caused by drought were a real threat and a constant reminder to the Israelites of their dependence on God to provide for them.

Although rain rarely falls in the summer season, winds from the Mediterranean Sea help to cool off the intense heat and bring heavy dew along the coastline. The dew provides the moisture required for agriculture during this season, especially for the growth of grapes. The Scriptures are full of references to dew because it played a major role in the life of the Israelites. Here is an example:

I WILL BE LIKE THE DEW TO ISRAEL; HE WILL BLOSSOM LIKE A LILY. LIKE A CEDAR OF LEBANON HE WILL SEND DOWN HIS ROOTS; HIS YOUNG SHOOTS WILL GROW. HIS SPLENDOR WILL BE LIKE AN OLIVE TREE, HIS FRAGRANCE LIKE A CEDAR OF LEBANON. MEN WILL DWELL AGAIN IN HIS SHADE. HE WILL FLOURISH LIKE THE GRAIN. HE WILL BLOSSOM LIKE A VINE, AND HIS FAME WILL BE LIKE THE WINE FROM LEBANON. —HOSEA 14:5-7

The chart below shows you the Hebrew months and how they correspond to our months, with a description of the climate and agricultural activities that happened in those months. The Jewish religious calendar, with their festivals and feasts, largely coincided with the cycle of agricultural activities. Some of the feasts have been included also. Notice that the Hebrew calendar year starts in the fall.

Calendar of Ancient Israel

HEBREW MONTH	OUR EQUIVALENT	CLIMATE AND AGRICULTURE	CROPS	JEWISH AGRICULTURAL-RELATED FESTIVAL
Nisan	March/April	Sunshine with very heavy winds; rains during this time are known as "latter rains" (James 5:7), which were important for nourishing the final growth of the wheat and barley crops before harvest.	Apricot and almond trees are showing off their splendor.	Barley harvest festivals: Feast of Passover (Ex. 11-14) and Feast of Unleavened Bread (Ex. 12:15-28), Feast of the Firstfruits (Lev. 23:9-14) (See Section 3 of Appendix)
Iyyar	April/May	Called the month of flowers and was the greenest and most beautiful month. Dry desert winds could blow in, melting snow and reviving vegetation. Barley harvesting begins.	Fruit trees, such as the peach, pomegranate, and olive, are in full blossom.	None
Sivan	May/June	Heat intensifies and rain stops for the next 5 months. Wheat harvesting begins.	Spring fruits, green almonds, apricots, and plums are ready to harvest. The grapevines are in blossom and are tended. (Song of Songs 2:11-13)	Wheat harvest festival: Feast of Shavu'ot/ Festival of Weeks/ Pentecost (Lev. 23:15-22)

HEBREW MONTH	OUR EQUIVALENT	CLIMATE AND AGRICULTURE	CROPS	JEWISH AGRICULTURAL-RELATED FESTIVAL
Tammaz	June/July	The land becomes parched and barren due to the intense heat.	Early grape harvest.	None
Ab	July/August	A refreshing westerly breeze begins to cool the summer heat.	Grapes, figs, and olives are ripe and ready to harvest.	None
Elul	August/ September	Hottest month of the year – can be as hot as 90 degrees in the shade.	Peaches, apples, pears, grapes, and figs ripen and are harvested.	None
Tishri	September/ October	The *siroccos* or desert winds blow, intensifying summer heat. The first showers begin, ending the long summer drought. Early plowing begins.	Figs and grapes are dried. Pomegranates and bananas ripen.	Fruit harvest festival: Feast of Succoth/Sukkot/ Booths (Lev. 23:33-44 – Feast of Tabernacles)
Merchesvan (Heshvan)	October/ November	Heavier rains fall, which are referred to in Scripture as the "former rains" (James 5:7). These rains loosen up hardened ground from the summer heat, making plowing possible. Beginning of wheat and barley sowing.	Grape, fig, and olive harvest are finishing. Sugarcane and dates ripen.	None
Chislev	November/ December	Still receiving former rain. Plowing and sowing wheat and barley in full swing.	None	None
Tebeth	December/ January	Late sowing still happening. Experiencing heavier rains and cooler weather. Grapevines are pruned.	Oranges, citrons, and lemons ripen.	None
Shebat (Shevat)	January/ February	Coldest month with dark, gloomy days and heavy rainfall.	Winter figs ripen.	New Year for Trees: Tu B'Shevat (Lev. 19:23-25)
Adar	February/ March	Combination of rainy and sunny days, a two-faced month. Late barley seeds are sown.	Almond trees begin to blossom.	None

Agricultural Techniques in Bible Times

The main crops of Israel were wheat and barley. Other crops mentioned in the Bible include lentils, flax, cucumbers, melons, and beans. Figs, pomegranates, grapes, and olives were also very plentiful and produced abundant fruit. Each portion of land was sectioned off according to the crop to be planted. Walls and hedges protected against the invasion of wild animals. There was much preparation necessary to ready the soil before seed planting. Stones and thorns were cleared from the land early in the year. The land was burned to destroy weeds. Ashes and manure were spread over the land to fertilize it, which would eventually be plowed into the dirt.

Since wheat was the most popular crop in Israel, we will look at the process of sowing and harvesting wheat.

Plowing

Plowing, or tilling up the soil, was done with a wooden stick, often a forked branch, which had a sharp spike attached to the end. It was either drawn along by people or animals, and this spike would cut into the ground about 3-4 inches deep. Usually the plow was pulled by two oxen (bulls) who were joined together by a yoke. It was forbidden through the law in Deuteronomy 22:10 to have an ox and a donkey yoked together. As the oxen pulled, the farmer walked behind, steering the plow with his left hand, and goading the oxen with his right hand (a *goad* was a pointed stick). He kept his eyes fixed directly ahead to make straight furrows, which were narrow grooves made in the ground, especially by a plow. The goad was used to prick the slow-moving oxen to keep them moving faster. The saying "kicking against the goad" came from this practice and defined a person who was stiff-necked and unwilling to go on the intended path. Areas where the plow was unable to go, such as steep hills or around trees, were plowed by hand using a tool like a hoe. Interesting note: The actual meaning of the word *acre* was the amount of land a yoke of oxen could plow in a day.

Planting or Sowing

To *sow* means to scatter seed over the ground (Matthew 13:3-8). This wasn't done in those days by sitting on a tractor, but by hand. The farmer would carry a container, pouch, or basket attached to his waist. He would take a handful of seed and with a sweeping stroke, cast the seed upon the prepared soil. Wheat seed would be sown in December and barley was sown a bit earlier. After the farmer scattered the seed, he would immediately plow over the field again to cover the seed with soil, preventing the birds from getting the seed. This was often done by dragging a branch or log behind a team of oxen. The following Scripture gives an example of this process:

> When a farmer plows for planting, does he plow continually? Does he keep on breaking up and harrowing the soil? When he has leveled the surface, does he not sow caraway and scatter cummin? Does he not plant wheat in its place, barley in its plot, and spelt in its field? His God instructs him and teaches him the right way. Caraway is not threshed with a sledge, nor is a cartwheel rolled over cummin; caraway is beaten out with a rod, and cummin with a stick. Grain must be ground to make bread; so one does not go on threshing it forever. Though he drives the wheels of his threshing cart over it, his horses do not grind it. All this also comes from the Lord Almighty, wonderful in counsel and magnificent in wisdom. —Isaiah 28:24-29

Harvesting or Reaping

To *harvest* means to gather in ripened crops. To *reap* means to cut down the grain. Before the crops were harvested, they first received the fullness of rain from the wet season. The barley crop was harvested mid-May and wheat was harvested in June. The harvest season lasted about 7 weeks and was the occasion for joyful festivities accompanied with great rejoicing and thanksgiving to God. (Refer to "Feast of the Firstfruits" in Section 2 for more information.) The reaping of the grain was done either by pulling it up by the roots or cutting it down with a *sickle* (handheld tool with a sharp, curved blade). The cut stalks would then be bound into sheaves or bundles. Revelation 14:14 describes Jesus holding a sickle in His hand ready to harvest the earth in the Final Harvest. "I looked, and there before me was a white cloud, and seated on the cloud was one 'like the son of man' with a crown of gold on his head and a sharp sickle in his hand."

Weeds and Wheat

The weeds mentioned in the parable in Matthew 13:24-30, 36-43 (see Lesson 30) were probably a type of weed grass called *darnel*. While the plants are young, darnel weeds resemble wheat. It is not until the darnel plants reach maturity that a difference can be seen in their seeds. Darnel seeds aren't good for much of anything except to be burned. Under certain conditions the seeds can actually become poisonous. The two plants—the darnel weeds and the wheat— are left to grow together because trying to uproot the darnel would harm the wheat.

Threshing

To *thresh* means to separate the kernels (grains) of wheat or barley from the stalk. These kernels were used to make bread; the stalks were not used for food. Threshing was done in several ways. Small amounts of bundles could be beaten with a stick causing the grain to separate from the stalk, as we read about Ruth doing in Ruth 2:17. Larger amounts of bundles were often threshed by spreading the sheaves on the threshing floor, where an ox would repeatedly walk over them. A threshing sledge, a platform of flat boards with an upturned front edge resembling a toboggan, was also used. This threshing sledge was weighted down with stones and was drawn by an animal (usually an ox). As the sledge was pulled over the wheat, the grains were separated from the stalks. Isaiah 41:15 says, "See, I will make you into a threshing sledge, new and sharp, with many teeth. You will thresh the mountains and crush them, and reduce the hills to chaff." Also, read the Isaiah 28 passage under the "Planting or Sowing" section.

Interesting note:

There was a law in Deuteronomy 25:4 which said, "Do not muzzle an ox while it is treading out the grain." In other words, do not prevent it from eating while it works. Paul, in 1 Corinthians 9:7-12, makes reference to this law. He is making a point to the Corinthians that those who labor full-time in the harvest should be able to receive support from those for whom they are laboring.

Winnowing

After the threshing is done, the worthless stalk (called *chaff*) and the good grains are lying together in piles. *Winnowing* is the process of separating the chaff from the good grain. The farmer would take a wooden shovel called a fan, scoop up both the grain and chaff, and throw them into the air. The useless chaff was lighter than the good grain and was blown away by the wind, while the heavier good grain fell onto a woven mat spread out on the ground. At the end of winnowing, the farmer had his mat piled up with good grain. The grain was then stored in granaries (large silos) or smaller storage jars until needed.

Since winnowing required a good strong breeze, it was usually done later in the evening when the winds were strongest. During the months of May through September a strong breeze blows off the Mediterranean, just in time for the harvest season.

The leftover wheat stalks were used as food and bedding for animals. The stalks were also used to weave baskets, or were mixed with mud to make bricks. After the stalks of wheat were cut and the winnowing was complete, the farmer would often allow the animals to graze on the stubble left in the field and to fertilize the field for next year's crops.

The wicked are referred to as "chaff" who will be burned in the Final Harvest (see Lesson 30): "His winnowing fork is in his hand, and he will clear his threshing floor, gathering his wheat into the barn and burning up the chaff with unquenchable fire" (Matthew 3:12).

> May they [my enemies] be like chaff before the wind, with the angel of the Lord driving them away. —Psalm 35:5

Vineyards

The climate of Israel was perfect for growing grape vineyards. Planting and care of a vineyard was intense and constant. Hillsides were used the most for planting vineyards, since they were not as suitable for other crops. However, vineyards were also planted in the plains and valleys. Terraces were built in the hillsides to hold more rain and prevent soil erosion. Stone walls and hedges were usually built around the vineyards to protect the grapes from animals and thieves.

A watchtower made of stone was also erected in the midst of the vineyard where a member of the family was constantly watching over the vineyard from the time of planting until harvest. Wild animals, fire, and robbers were constant threats to the grapes. During the harvest, the owner of the vineyard would often stay in a booth to protect his valuable crop.

Grapevines required thorough annual pruning, digging, thinning, supporting fruit clusters, and irrigation. The vines were allowed to run along the ground, or sometimes they might climb a nearby tree. This was a time of celebration where families would make booths (temporary shelters) in the vineyard in which they would live until the completion of the harvest.

The grapes were harvested in August or September. Grapes were tasted to determine their ripeness. When harvest time came, grapes were crushed by the harvester's feet in winepresses hewn out of rock. The extract from the grapes flowed through stone channels into lower vats that were dug into the soft limestone of the hillside. Teams of workers would replace each other during the treading process. Singing and chanting accompanied by music kept them energized and distracted from the demands of the treading. It was during this harvest that the Jewish festival Tu B'Av was celebrated. Single women would go out into the vineyards in white dresses and dance in the hope of attracting husbands.

Fresh grapes were eaten in large amounts during the harvest season and dried into clusters of raisins for future use. The juice boiled down to make a thick syrup, which was called *honey*. Wine or "new wine" was the chief product of the vineyard.

The Song of the Vineyard

> I will sing for the one I love a song about his vineyard: My loved one had a vineyard on a fertile hillside. He dug it up and cleared it of stones and planted it with the choicest vines. He built a watchtower in it and cut out a winepress as well. Then he looked for a crop of good grapes, but it yielded only bad fruit.
>
> —Isaiah 5:1-2

Feast of the Firstfruits

The Lord said to Moses, "Speak to the Israelites and say to them: 'When you enter the land I am going to give you and you reap its harvest, bring to the priest a sheaf of the first grain you harvest. He is to wave the sheaf before the Lord so it will be accepted on your behalf.' " —Leviticus 23:9-11

The Feast of Firstfruits was held at the time of the first grain harvest, occurring at the time of Passover in the month of Nisan. It is also called the "Waving of the Sheaves." The firstfruits are the first parts of the harvest to ripen. Nothing is supposed to be eaten of the harvest until the feast is completed. In ancient days, this feast was quite an elaborate ceremony. The priest would meet a group of Jewish worshippers at the edge of the city and would lead them up the Temple Mount. As this progression moved along carrying their offerings, the priest led the people in songs of praise with music and dance. When they arrived at the temple, the priest would take the sheaves, lift some of them up, and wave them around before the Lord. This was done to first thank and honor God for His provision of the harvest and for His continued blessing on the crops yet to come.

In 1 Corinthians 15:20-23, Christ is referred to as the firstfruit of those who will be raised from the dead. Jesus—the first to be resurrected—is our firstfruit, the promise of the blessing waiting for us at the final great harvest. When He comes, we too shall be harvested unto the Lord.

Section 4

FLOWERS OF THE BIBLE

Because the Bible is not a botany book, the names of species of flowers are different from how we know them today, making it difficult to identify these flowers mentioned in Scripture. Botanists have made very intelligent guesses. The flowers mentioned below are definitely found in the Holy Land and could easily be one of those mentioned in the verses listed after their description.

ANEMONE—This is part of the buttercup family. These plants are perennial herbs with elongated flower stems, each bearing one or several flowers. They come in shades of red, pink, purple, blue, and white, but red is the most common and perhaps most striking color. They are planted in October and will bloom in May and June. They are often called windflowers because they like windward places. These were probably some of the flowers Jesus referred to in His Sermon on the Mount. These flowers open in the morning and close at night. Scripture reference: Matthew 6:28

BLUE OR YELLOW FLAG IRIS—These irises are the most common wild irises in the world. They grow wild in the Holy Lands and are often found gracing the banks of streams and waterways. The blooms of these handsome flowers have been admired throughout recorded history. Each stem grows 3-4 feet tall. The unique blooms have a combination of erect and drooping petals. The iris blooms in late spring to early summer. Because this plant is resilient and able to survive great dry periods or immersion in water, it has become the symbol of the undefeated and triumphant believer in the face of trials. Scripture reference: Hosea 14:5

CYCLAMEN—One variety of this plant is known as the Alpine Violet. It grows wild in stone walls and can be found nestled among rocks and crevices. It is common to see it growing along the roadways of Israel today. It blooms for a long time—from December until April if kept cool. The blossoms range from vivid pink to white and look like tiny butterflies clinging to the top of the plant's slender stem. They have also been known as "Solomon's Crown." Scripture reference: Luke 12:27

HYACINTH—This is one of the most aromatic and therefore favorite flowers of the Bible. During blooming season these gorgeous flowers blanket the hillsides in Galilee. They were cultivated by the world's earliest gardeners. The bulbs of this plant were very expensive and sought after because of their fragrant quality. The plant bears deep blue, highly fragrant spikes with sword-shaped leaves. Today, these flowers are found in brilliant colors from blue and red to bright pink and orange. Scripture reference: Song of Songs 6:2-3

MADONNA LILY—This magnificent lily is one of the oldest cultivated lilies, possibly from as early as 1,500 years before Christ. This incredibly fragrant lily blooms in the summer and boasts of pure white flowers with yellow throats standing tall on 3-5 foot stems. In the evening they are breathtaking in a garden, gleaming in the moonlight. This Madonna Lily is the traditional Easter lily and has been the symbol of purity for over 3,000 years. Scripture reference: Song of Songs 6:2, Hosea 14:5

NARCISSUS (DAFFODIL)—The narcissus native to the Holy Land has a central trumpet-shaped lemon-yellow corona (crown) surrounded by a ring of white petals. It has long, slender leaves and a bulbous root. In its natural habitat it blooms in November. It can be found growing in the damp soil of the plains as well as among the rocks and shrubs of the hill country and into the Negev Desert. Daffodils are beautiful to look at but are poisonous if eaten. Scripture reference: Matthew 6:28

SAFFRON CROCUS—This delightful flower blooms in late autumn and is a tiny plant with several narrow leaves and one or more large, bluish-lilac flowers. It is a very fragrant flower. When plucked and dried it yields a very special, valuable spice called saffron. Saffron has many uses. Historically, its medicinal qualities were said to heal everything from rheumatism to measles. It has been used for dyes, perfumes, and flavoring foods. It is known as the most expensive spice in the world. Scripture reference: Song of Songs 4:14

STAR OF BETHLEHEM— Just as it did in ancient times, this flower still grows wild today in the Holy Land. You can see this joyful little flower dotting fields, hillsides, and other stony places with its bright white, cheerful blossoms. Numerous white, lily-like star-shaped flowers bloom in the spring on stalks 10-12 inches high. Strangely, this flower was known as "dove's dung" probably due to the way they bloom in groupings resembling white droppings from doves. The bulbs were eaten raw or cooked and were considered a tasty, wholesome food. The bulbs are still eaten in the East and are roasted like chestnuts. Scripture reference: 2 Kings 6:25

TULIP—Recorded history tells us that tulips were cultivated ages ago in Turkey. The word *tulip* comes from the Persian word for *turban,* which originated from the common Turkish custom of wearing flowers in the folds of the turban. There is a wild tulip known as the Mountain Tulip, which is native to the Holy Land and bears a single, bright red flower. It is known far and wide for its striking beauty. The Mountain Tulip's single large crimson flower blooms in the spring and lasts only a week or so. Scripture reference: Song of Songs 2:12

Section 5

TREES OF THE BIBLE

ACACIA TREE—The Acacia tree, also known as the Shittah tree, is one of the thorny trees found in the Holy Land. Acacia trees are sweet smelling with yellow flowers and soft, green leaves. It can grow quite large and has thorns growing from its spreading branches. The bark is gnarly, black, and rough in texture. The wood from this tree was used to build the ark and various other pieces of furniture for the tabernacle. The wood of this tree is a beautiful orange-colored wood that darkens with age. It is said to be insect-resistant. Scripture references: Isaiah 41:19; Exodus 25:5, 10-13, 23, 28; 26:15

ALEPPO PINE TREE—This pine is native to the Mediterranean region. Its Hebrew name is the "Jerusalem Pine." It is probably also referred to as the fir tree in the Bible. It is a small- to medium- size tree reaching about 65 feet tall. The bark is orange-red in color. Its needles are yellowish green, and they bear cones with seeds in them. It is a very popular tree for ornamental and lumber uses, and is highly valued due to its heat and drought tolerance. Its *resin* (sap) was used in Egypt for embalming. Pines are known for their wonderful fresh scent. Scripture references: Isaiah 60:13, Psalm 104:17, Hosea 14:8, Ezekiel 31:8, Isaiah 55:13

CEDARS OF LEBANON—This tree was found at higher altitudes in Lebanon and Turkey. It was valued for being one of the most aromatic and resistant types of wood known. The wood from these awesome cedars was so strong and beautiful that it was greatly used in ancient times for building houses, temples, and ships. It is an evergreen and can grow as tall as 130 feet! It has an unusual shape to it—very wide with branches that grow straight out and a flattened top. They symbolize strength and magnificence. These amazing trees used to be very abundant in the Holy Land, but are now rare. There is, however, an extensive amount of replanting of these magnificent trees occurring in Turkey. The Lebanon cedar is mentioned 75 times in the Bible. It is the national emblem of Lebanon and is seen on the Lebanese Flag. Scripture references: Psalm 92:12, Hosea 14:5-6, Amos 2:9, Psalm 29:5, Psalm 104:16

CYPRESS TREE—This tree grows abundantly on the mountains in Israel and can survive up to 2,000 years or more. These evergreens can grow to the height of 90 feet and are candle-shaped in appearance. Its wood, yellowish-red in color, is hard, fragrant, and durable, lasting for centuries. It resists rotting even after prolonged soaking in water. Because of this quality, many believe this was the wood from which Noah's Ark was made. The wood of the cypress tree has a wonderful cedar scent and contains essential oils that make it very fragrant. Therefore, it was customary to plant these trees near houses, churches, or cemeteries where they were thought to purify and freshen the air. Scripture references: Isaiah 44:14, Isaiah 60:13, Ezekiel 27:6, Genesis 6:14

FIG TREE—The fig tree is one of the most valuable resources in Israel and is among the earliest cultivated crops. Figs are recorded to have been grown 11,400 years ago. The fig tree can grow over 33 feet tall. It produces two, sometimes three crops of figs each year. In Biblical times, figs were used medicinally and were a valuable food because they could be dried for long-term storage. Figs were used as a sign of peace and prosperity. Scripture references: Genesis 3:7, Mark 11:13-14, Isaiah 34:4, Proverbs 27:18, Joel 2:22, Judges 9:10-11

MYRTLE—The myrtle is a shrub with extremely fragrant leaves and beautiful white flowers. The Hebrew name means "sweetness." Its scent was considered more exquisite than the rose and was used to make wreaths of crowns for kings. To the ancient Jews it was a symbol of peace and justice. The Jews collected the boughs of this plant to make booths during the Feast of Tabernacles. Today the leaves are used as a spice and all parts of the plant are dried to make perfume. Scripture references: Isaiah 41:19, Nehemiah 8:15, Isaiah 55:13, Zechariah 1:7-11

OAK TREE—Oak trees are deciduous trees; they shed their leaves during one season. They can live as long as 200 years or more. The mighty oak tree is symbolic of being strong, enduring, and steadfast. They were often used to mark boundaries because of their longevity and ability to endure. Their great stature made them ideal to serve as landmarks for meeting places or for marking a spot to bury treasure. These common practices are mentioned in the Bible. They commonly reach a height of 60 feet. The oak takes 70-80 years before it begins to produce an abundant amount of acorns. Its extremely hard and dense wood makes it ideal for building material and firewood. The leaves and bark of the tree can be used for medicinal purposes. Jesus probably taught under big, sprawling oak trees. They offer shade and inspiration as we sit beneath them. Scripture references: Genesis 35:4, 2 Samuel 18:9, Joshua 24:26, Isaiah 6:13, Psalm 29:9, Isaiah 1:29-30

OLIVE TREE—The olive tree is native to the Holy Land, and according to historians, began to be cultivated around 4,000 B.C. Olive trees range from 10-40 feet tall. It is a broad-leafed evergreen with leathery, lance-shaped, dark green leaves. The fruit—the olive—was used as food and for lamp oil. The olive tree is slow growing, taking 7 years to mature, but very productive throughout its life. It can live and produce for 2,000 years and is a symbol of tenacity and fruitfulness. The olive tree blooms between April and June with perfumed flowers located where the previous year's leaves were. The olive wood is the hardiest, heaviest, and most solid wood known to man and therefore makes for good building material and beautiful carvings. The olive tree has been a symbol of hope, beauty, peace, and fertility. The dove returned to Noah in the ark with an olive branch. Scripture references: Genesis 8:11, Jeremiah 11:16, Judges 9:8-15, Revelation 11:4, Isaiah 17:6, Habakkuk 3:17

PALM TREE—The date-palm is characteristic of the Holy Land. It is one of the oldest fruit trees in the world. It is described as flourishing, tall, and upright. Its branches are a symbol of victory, especially victory over death. It rises very tall, 40 to 80 feet, on a slender trunk with feathery branches of snow-like, pale-green fronds from 6-12 feet long. Its fruit— dates—are sweet and delicious. The palm tree lives to be about 150 years old. The whole land of Israel was known as the "land of the palms." Branches of these palms were carried for the Feast of Tabernacles and the crowds were waving palm branches when Jesus entered Jerusalem riding on the colt of a donkey. King Solomon's Temple was decorated with carvings of palm trees. Scripture reference: Psalm 92:12, John 12:13, Leviticus 23:39-40, Numbers 33:9, 1 Kings 6:32

Section 6

THE GREATEST PLAN ON EARTH

Plan of Salvation

God desired for you to be His child even before He created the earth. That is why you were created—to be God's child. Ephesians 1:4-5 says, "In love he predestined us to be adopted as his sons through Jesus Christ, in accordance with his pleasure and will." First John 3:1 says, "How great is the love the Father has lavished on us, that we should be called children of God!"

God gives His children the freedom to make choices (free will). He doesn't want a bunch of "robots" programmed to love Him. He wants us to *choose* to love Him. But our free will can be a problem. When God created Adam and Eve, He allowed them the choice of whether to obey Him or not. They chose *not* to obey, and mankind has been stuck with this rebellious nature ever since. "For all have sinned and fall short of the glory of God" (Romans 3:23). A rebellious nature causes us to sin, and sin *separates* us from God, because God Himself is completely sinless. Sin leads to death: "For the wages of sin is death, but the gift of God is eternal life in Christ Jesus our Lord" (Romans 6:23).

God understood our sin problem. He knew that we were unable to get rid of our rebellious nature on our own. Because He is the most perfect, loving Father, He did for us what we could not do for ourselves. He sent His flawless Son, Jesus Christ, to pay the penalty for our sins. Jesus came to earth as a sinless man and took upon Himself our sin nature as He died on a Cross. Our sinful nature died with Him on that Cross. Three days later, Jesus arose from the dead, powerful and victorious! Here's the really good news! "If we have been united with him [Christ] like this in his death, we will certainly also be united with him in his resurrection" (Romans 6:5). If we died with Him, then we shall also live with Him. We can now experience the fullness of life, powerful and victorious over sin, as children of God through the resurrected life of Jesus Christ.

To receive the gift of salvation, first admit that you are trapped in this sin nature and that you need Jesus to save you. Take the free will that God has given you and make a choice—the greatest choice you will ever make—to live with and for Christ. Choose to turn from the old, sinful nature, which leads to death, and make Jesus your life. This is called *repentance*. "Repent, then, and turn to God, so that your sins may be wiped out" (Acts 3:19). Choose to live this way every day. "Count yourselves dead to sin but alive to God in Christ Jesus" (Romans 6:11). Next, believe and receive! "Yet to all who received him, to those who believed in his name, he gave the right to become children of God—children born not of natural descent, nor of human decision or a husband's will, but born of God" (John 1:12-13). By faith we must trust Jesus and receive Him as our Savior and Lord. It's that simple.

Now that you are a child of God Almighty, Creator of Heaven and Earth, you have an *incredible* inheritance:

1. You have eternal life with Christ now and forever. (John 3:16)
2. Your sins are forgiven. (Colossians 1:13-14)
3. You are holy and righteous through the blood of Jesus. When God sees you, He sees the life of His perfect Son. (Philippians 3:9)
4. You now have Christ's life living in you through the Holy Spirit, who is your Helper sent from God. (John 14:16)
5. You can be assured of your salvation. When Christ died on the Cross, He proclaimed, "It is finished." This means He has done everything necessary for your salvation. You do not need to earn it or work for it. You only have to believe and let Christ live His life in you (Ephesians 2:8-9). By faith you have received this wonderful new life in Christ. Now by faith, let His life live through you!

Here are some simple steps to do once you have accepted Christ into your heart:

- Tell someone else (preferably another Christian) about the commitment you just made to the Lord.
- Find a church that teaches the Bible and attend it regularly. Get involved in a home Bible study group.
- Get water baptized. Talk to your pastor and parents about this.
- Seek out other Christians in your school or at your work or in other places and develop new friendships.

Enjoy your relationship with Jesus—your very closest Forever Friend!

Collect all of our Violet products!

A Life of Faith: Violet Travilla Series

Book One —Violet's Hidden Doubts....................... ISBN: 1-928749-17-8
Book Two —Violet's Amazing Summer.................. ISBN: 1-928749-18-6
Book Three —Violet's Turning Point......................... ISBN: 1-928749-19-4
Book Four —Violet's Bold Mission.......................... ISBN: 1-928749-20-8
Book Five —Violet's Perplexing Puzzles .... ISBN: 1-928749-21-6
Book Six —Violet's Bumpy Ride........................... ISBN: 1-928749-22-4
Book Seven —Violet's Defiant Daughter..................... ISBN: 1-928749-23-2
Book Eight —Violet's Foreign Intrigue .... ISBN: 1-928749-24-0
Violet's Life Lessons: Growing Toward God .... ISBN: 1-928749-62-3

For more information, write to

Mission City Press at 202 Seond Ave. South,
Franklin, Tennessee 37064
or visit our Web Site at:

www.alifeoffaith.com

Collect all of our Elsie products!

Dear Elsie
Elsie's
Life Lessons
Walking In the Fruit of the Spirit
ELSIE'S
Christmas Party

A Life of Faith: Elsie Dinsmore Series

Book One —Elsie's Endless Wait............................ISBN: 1-928749-01-1 *
Book Two —Elsie's Impossible Choice..................ISBN: 1-928749-02-X *
Book Three —Elsie's New Life.................................ISBN: 1-928749-03-8
Book Four —Elsie's Stolen Heart...........................ISBN: 1-928749-04-6
Book Five —Elsie's True Love...............................ISBN: 1-928749-05-4
Book Six —Elsie's Troubled Times.......................ISBN: 1-928749-06-2
Book Seven —Elsie's Tender Mercies.......................ISBN: 1-928749-07-0
Book Eight —Elsie's Great Hope.............................ISBN: 1-928749-08-9
Dear Elsie: Answers to Questions Girls Ask............ISBN: 1-928749-55-0
Elsie's Life Lessons (A Study Guide)........................ISBN: 1-928749-51-8
Elsie's Christmas Party (A Gift/Activity Book)........ISBN: 1-928749-52-6
Elsie's Daily Diary: A Personal Journal for Girls........ ISBN: 1-928749-50-X
Elsie's Paper Doll Collection.....................................ISBN: 1-928749-33-X

*** Now Available as a Dramatized Audiobook!**

Elsie's Endless Wait—Dramatized Audiobook............ ISBN: 1-928749-76-3
Elsie's Impossible Choice—Dramatized Audiobook.... ISBN: 1-928749-78-X

Collect all of our Millie products!

A Life of Faith: Millie Keith Series

Book One — Millie's Unsettled Season .... ISBN: 1-928749-09-7 *
Book Two — Millie's Courageous Days .... ISBN: 1-928749-10-0 *
Book Three — Millie's Remarkable Journey .... ISBN: 1-928749-11-9
Book Four — Millie's Faithful Heart .... ISBN: 1-928749-12-7
Book Five — Millie's Steadfast Love .... ISBN: 1-928749-13-5
Book Six — Millie's Grand Adventure .... ISBN: 1-928749-14-3
Book Seven — Millie's Reluctant Sacrifice .... ISBN: 1-928749-15-1
Book Eight — Millie's Fiery Trial .... ISBN: 1-928749-16-X
Millie's Life Lessons: Adventures in Trusting God ..... ISBN: 1-928749-57-7
Millie's Daily Diary: A Personal Journal for Girls ..... ISBN: 1-928749-56-9
Dear Millie: Answers to Questions Girls Ask .... ISBN: 1-928749-59-3
Millie's Prayer Projects: Creative Ways to Pray .... ISBN: 1-928749-58-5
Millie's Paper Doll Collection .... ISBN: 1-928749-34-8

*** Now Available as a Dramatized Audiobook!**
Millie's Unsettled Season—Dramatized Audiobook .... ISBN: 1-928749-77-1
Millie's Courageous Days—Dramatized Audiobook ... ISBN: 1-928749-79-8

A Life of Faith: Laylie Colbert

Laylie's Daring Quest .... ISBN: 1-928749-35-6

Collect all of our Kathleen products!

A Life of Faith: Millie Keith Series

Book One —Kathleen's Shaken Dreams ....ISBN: 1-928749-25-9
Book Two —Kathleen's Unforgettable Winter.......ISBN: 1-928749-26-7
Book Three —Kathleen's Abiding Hope ....ISBN: 1-928749-27-5
Book Four —Kathleen's Enduring Faith.................ISBN: 1-928749-28-3

SEEDS FOR YOUR NEW LIFE

IN CHRIST, YOU ARE:

a child of God—John 1:12-13
a child of light—Ephesians 5:8
fruitful, fresh, and flourishing —Psalm 92:13-14
a fountain of living water—John 7:37-38
a new creation—2 Corinthians 5:17
renewed daily—2 Corinthians 4:16
chosen to be holy and blameless —Ephesians 1:4
created to do good works—Ephesians 2:10
alive in Christ—Ephesians 2:5
positioned in a victorious place —Ephesians 2:6
appointed to go and bear fruit—John 15:16

SEEDS FOR YOUR GROWTH

- Examine your faith—2 Corinthians 13:5
- Repent and be refreshed—Acts 3:19
- Seek first His kingdom and righteousness —Matthew 6:33
- Know the fruit of the spirit—Galatians 5:22-23
- Test your thoughts—Philippians 4:8
- Do God's will—1 Thessalonians 5:16-18
- Stay rooted in God's love—Ephesians 3:17-19
- Trust God to complete His growth in you —Philippians 1:6
- By faith receive Christ's life—Colossians 2:6-7
- Live in harmony with others—Colossians 3:12-13
- Walk in the light of Christ—John 8:12
- Find rest for your soul—Matthew 11:28-30
- Confess your sins—1 John 1:9
- Encourage one another—Hebrews 10:24-25
- Live right by the grace of God—Titus 2:11-14

SEEDS FOR YOUR HARVEST

- God's Word accomplishes His purpose —Isaiah 55:9-11
- You will bear fruit in every good work —Colossians 1:10
- Do not grow weary—Galatians 6:9
- You are called into the harvest —Matthew 28:18-20
- Shine on your harvest field —Matthew 5:14
- God will give you all you need for harvesting —2 Corinthians 9:8
- The fields are ripe for harvest —John 4:35-36
- God supplies your seed and multiplies your harvest—2 Corinthians 9:10
- Weeping leads to reaping—Psalm 126:5-6
- Harvesters have beautiful feet —Romans 10:14-15

SEEDS FOR YOUR NEW LIFE

THROUGH CHRIST, YOU HAVE . . .

the perfect love of Christ and the Father —John 15:9

been redeemed and forgiven —Ephesians 1:7

been blessed with every spiritual blessing —Ephesians 1:3

the promise of the Holy Spirit—Ephesians 1:13

the power of God mightily working in you —Ephesians 1:19

an inheritance of heavenly riches —Ephesians 1:18

God's immeasurable grace and kindness —Ephesians 2:7

the free gift of salvation—Ephesians 2:8

all that you need spiritually—2 Peter 1:3

the life of Christ living in you—Galatians 2:20

SEED PACKETS of TRUTH

MORE SEEDS FOR YOUR HARVEST

- You are a herald of glad tidings —Isaiah 40:9
- Sow generously; reap generously —2 Corinthians 9:6
- Give it your all; your labor is not in vain —1 Corinthians 15:58
- Bear fruit to glorify God—John 15:8
- Remain in the Vine—John 15:4-5
- Be faithful with a few things —Matthew 25:21
- Give freely and gain even more —Proverbs 11:24
- Keep your focus—Luke 9:62
- Be prepared for the final harvest —2 Peter 3:13-14

SEEDS FOR YOUR STORMS

- Lean on God's love & faithfulness —Psalm 57:10
- Put your confidence in the Lord —Jeremiah 17:7-8
- God gives guidance, strength, and sustenance —Isaiah 58:11
- The Lord is your strength and your song —Isaiah 12:2-3
- Joyful fruit comes from trials—James 1:2-4
- Your storm will not last forever—Psalm 30:5
- Christ overcomes your storm—John 16:33
- Suffering yields good fruit—Romans 5:3
- God will make you strong, firm, and steadfast —1 Peter 5:10
- Discipline produces a harvest of righteousness —Hebrews 12:11
- Your wilderness will bloom—Isaiah 35:1-2
- You can do all things through Christ —Philippians 4:13
- God will never leave you—Hebrews 13:5

Seeds for Your New Life

In Christ, you are:

a child of God—John 1:12-13
a child of light—Ephesians 5:8
fruitful, fresh, and flourishing
—Psalm 92:13-14
a fountain of living water—John 7:37-38
a new creation—2 Corinthians 5:17
renewed daily—2 Corinthians 4:16
chosen to be holy and blameless
—Ephesians 1:4
created to do good works—Ephesians 2:10
alive in Christ—Ephesians 2:5
positioned in a victorious place
—Ephesians 2:6
appointed to go and bear fruit—John 15:16

Seeds for Your Growth

- Examine your faith—2 Corinthians 13:5
- Repent and be refreshed—Acts 3:19
- Seek first His kingdom and righteousness —Matthew 6:33
- Know the fruit of the spirit—Galatians 5:22-23
- Test your thoughts—Philippians 4:8
- Do God's will—1 Thessalonians 5:16-18
- Stay rooted in God's love—Ephesians 3:17-19
- Trust God to complete His growth in you —Philippians 1:6
- By faith receive Christ's life—Colossians 2:6-7
- Live in harmony with others—Colossians 3:12-13
- Walk in the light of Christ—John 8:12
- Find rest for your soul—Matthew 11:28-30
- Confess your sins—1 John 1:9
- Encourage one another—Hebrews 10:24-25
- Live right by the grace of God—Titus 2:11-14

Seeds for Your Harvest

- God's Word accomplishes His purpose —Isaiah 55:9-11
- You will bear fruit in every good work —Colossians 1:10
- Do not grow weary—Galatians 6:9
- You are called into the harvest —Matthew 28:18-20
- Shine on your harvest field —Matthew 5:14
- God will give you all you need for harvesting —2 Corinthians 9:8
- The fields are ripe for harvest —John 4:35-36
- God supplies your seed and multiplies your harvest—2 Corinthians 9:10
- Weeping leads to reaping—Psalm 126:5-6
- Harvesters have beautiful feet —Romans 10:14-15

SEEDS FOR YOUR NEW LIFE

THROUGH CHRIST, YOU HAVE . . .

the perfect love of Christ and the Father —John 15:9

been redeemed and forgiven —Ephesians 1:7

been blessed with every spiritual blessing —Ephesians 1:3

the promise of the Holy Spirit—Ephesians 1:13

the power of God mightily working in you —Ephesians 1:19

an inheritance of heavenly riches —Ephesians 1:18

God's immeasurable grace and kindness —Ephesians 2:7

the free gift of salvation—Ephesians 2:8

all that you need spiritually—2 Peter 1:3

the life of Christ living in you—Galatians 2:20

MORE SEEDS FOR YOUR HARVEST

- You are a herald of glad tidings —Isaiah 40:9
- Sow generously; reap generously —2 Corinthians 9:6
- Give it your all; your labor is not in vain —1 Corinthians 15:58
- Bear fruit to glorify God—John 15:8
- Remain in the Vine—John 15:4-5
- Be faithful with a few things —Matthew 25:21
- Give freely and gain even more —Proverbs 11:24
- Keep your focus—Luke 9:62
- Be prepared for the final harvest —2 Peter 3:13-14

SEEDS FOR YOUR STORMS

- Lean on God's love & faithfulness —Psalm 57:10
- Put your confidence in the Lord —Jeremiah 17:7-8
- God gives guidance, strength, and sustenance —Isaiah 58:11
- The Lord is your strength and your song —Isaiah 12:2-3
- Joyful fruit comes from trials—James 1:2-4
- Your storm will not last forever—Psalm 30:5
- Christ overcomes your storm—John 16:33
- Suffering yields good fruit—Romans 5:3
- God will make you strong, firm, and steadfast —1 Peter 5:10
- Discipline produces a harvest of righteousness —Hebrews 12:11
- Your wilderness will bloom—Isaiah 35:1-2
- You can do all things through Christ —Philippians 4:13
- God will never leave you—Hebrews 13:5